Downtown 3

English for Work and Life

Workbook

JOHN CHAPMAN

THOMSON

HEINLE

Australia • Canada • Mexico • Singapore • Spain • United Kingdom • United States

THOMSON

HEINLE

Downtown 3
English for Work and Life
Workbook
John Chapman

Publisher, Academic ESL: James W. Brown
Executive Editor, Dictionaries & Adult ESL: Sherrise Roehr
Director of Content Development: Anita Raducanu
Director of Product Marketing: Amy Mabley
Senior Field Marketing Manager: Donna Lee Kennedy
Editorial Assistant: Katherine Reilly
Senior Production Editor: Maryellen E. Killeen
Senior Print Buyer: Mary Beth Hennebury

Development Editor: Kasia McNabb
Design and Composition: Parkwood Composition
Project Management: Tünde Dewey
Cover Design: Lori Stuart
Cover Art: Jean-François Allaux
Printer: P. A. Hutchison

For more information contact Thomson Heinle, 25 Thomson Place, Boston, MA 02210 USA, or visit our Internet site at elt.thomson.com

ISBN 10: 0-8384-5327-9
ISBN 13: 978-0-8384-5327-8

Contents

1. Introductions 1
Lesson 1: Nice to Meet You 2
Lesson 2: Neighbors 5
Lesson 3: Erika Needs a Job 7
Review 9

2. Love and Marriage 10
Lesson 1: Newlyweds 11
Lesson 2: Changes 13
Lesson 3: Career Ladders 15
Review 18

3. Family Economics 19
Lesson 1: Plans and Predictions 20
Lesson 2: Money 22
Lesson 3: Hopes and Dreams 25
Review 27

4. The Community 28
Lesson 1: Community Services 29
Lesson 2: Working Together 31
Lesson 3: Neighborhood Jobs 33
Review 36

5. People and Places 37
Lesson 1: Have You Ever … ? 38
Lesson 2: The Best Places 40
Lesson 3: Erika's Job Interview 42
Review 45

6. Housing 46
Lesson 1: Homes 47
Lesson 2: Bills 50
Lesson 3: Erika's New Job 52
Review 54

7. Health and Safety 55
Lesson 1: Staying Healthy 56
Lesson 2: The Doctor's Office 58
Lesson 3: Safety 61
Review 63

8. Travel and Transportation 64
Lesson 1: Travel Plans 65
Lesson 2: Getting There 67
Lesson 3: Buying a Car 69
Review 72

9. Government and the Law 73
Lesson 1: The Law 74
Lesson 2: Citizenship 77
Lesson 3: History and Government 79
Review 81

10. Work 82
Lesson 1: Working Together 83
Lesson 2: Rules at Work 86
Lesson 3: Job Performance 88
Review 90

Introductions

Vocabulary

1 **Circle the correct word or words in each sentence.**

1. I need to ((find) / help) a job.

2. She will (**move to / meet**) a new apartment next week.

3. I never see my family and I (**watch / miss**) them.

4. They are (**doing / having**) dinner at home.

5. I want to (**do / have**) a party.

6. He will (**make / meet**) his new neighbors.

7. He will (**miss / make**) some new friends.

8. He needs to (**read / practice**) his English.

9. I always (**listen / sound**) to music at work.

10. I never (**look / watch**) TV at work.

2 **Fill in the blanks with words from the box.**

feel	unemployed	newspaper	homesick
married	sounds	~~neighborhood~~	single

1. I don't like my _____neighborhood._____ I don't have any friends there.

2. I love my home country, Haiti. I am _____ for it.

3. American music _____ different from Haitian music.

4. I don't have a wife. I am _____.

5. I want to get _____.

6. Then I will _____ better.

7. I want to get a job, but right now I am _____.

8. I read the _____ every day.

Nice to Meet You

① Match the questions and answers. Write them under the appropriate picture.

How is she feeling?   ~~The round one.~~

When does she get up?   She's studying.

Who has an umbrella?   They do.

Where is she?   She's happy.

What is she doing?   She's at a health club.

~~Which cake does she want?~~   At 6:00.

1.

A: *Which cake does she want?*

B: *The round one.*

2.

A: _____

B: _____

3.

A: _____

B: _____

4.

A: _____

B: _____

5.

A: _____

B: _____

6.

A: _____

B: _____

2 Cross out the incorrect verb. Then write the correct verb in the blank. Use the words from the box.

| play | take | find | ~~go~~ | feel | cook | ride | meet | watch | listen |

1. I like to ~~listen~~ to the movies. _____go_____
2. Let's make some photographs. _____
3. I need to think a new job. _____
4. We want to talk the new neighbors. _____
5. We usually see TV in the evening. _____
6. I do my bicycle to school every day. _____
7. I take dinner at home every night. _____
8. Let's go soccer after school. _____
9. When I have dinner, I will find better. _____
10. I hear to music on my CD-ROM player. _____

3 Rearrange the words to complete the sentences correctly.

1. I have class at 9:00, ____and so do you.____ (do / so / you / and)
2. We have a test tomorrow, _____. (they / and / too /do)
3. My friends use their computers every day, _____. (so / I / and / do)
4. They study every night, _____. (and / do / we / so)
5. I always come to class early, _____. (and / she / too / does)

4 Complete the sentences to show positive agreement. Describe yourself and other people in your life. Use ...do, too; ...does, too; so do..., and so does....

Example: _My brother loves pizza_, and _____so does my sister._____

1. _____, and _____.
2. _____, and _____.
3. _____, and _____.
4. _____, and _____.
5. _____, and _____.

⑤ Number the lines of each conversation in the correct order.

1.

____ I'm in 2-E. How about you Jack?

____ Which apartment do you live in, Tim?

__1__ Hi. My name is Jack.

____ Hi, Jack. Nice to meet you. I'm Tim.

____ I live in 4-F.

2.

____ It's Barbara.

____ She's not working. She's looking for a job.

____ I met our new neighbor today.

____ What does she do?

____ Oh, I see.

____ Oh? What's her name?

3.

____ I'm from Los Angeles.

____ Where are you from, Patty?

____ Hi. I'm your new neighbor. My name is Lisa.

____ Nice to meet you, Lisa. I'm Patty.

____ New York. How about you?

____ That's interesting.

4.

____ Yes, she is. And she has two children.

____ Is she married?

____ I met a new neighbor today.

____ I met Maria. She's very nice.

____ Who did you meet?

____ Oh, really? That's interesting.

5.

____ And where is Thomas from?

____ Oh? What is his name?

____ Thomas. He's very nice.

____ He's from Canada.

____ I met the man in apartment 7-B.

6.

____ I'm Teddy.

____ Hello. I'm Gail. What's your name?

____ 4-L.

____ Hi, I'm your new neighbor.

____ What apartment do you live in, Teddy?

Neighbors

① **Read the chart. Then complete the sentences with the correct adverb of frequency from the box.**

	Monday	*Tuesday*	*Wednesday*	*Thursday*	*Friday*	*Saturday*	*Sunday*
CLARA	reads magazines	reads magazines	reads magazines	reads magazines	reads magazines	reads magazines	reads magazines
	watches TV	watches TV					plays cards
JOE	plays the guitar		plays the guitar	plays the guitar	plays the guitar	plays the guitar	plays the guitar
		reads the newspaper					reads the newspaper
	goes to the movies	goes to the movies	goes to the movies	goes to the movies	goes to the movies	goes to the movies	

sometimes	always	never	usually	often

1. Joe ___*often*___ plays the guitar.
2. Clara _____ plays cards.
3. Joe _____ reads the newspaper.
4. Joe _____ reads magazines.
5. Clara _____ reads magazines.
6. Clara _____ plays the guitar.
7. Joe _____ goes to the movies.
8. Clara _____ watches TV.

② **Describe things you and other people in your life do. Use *always, sometimes, usually, often,* and *never.***

1. _____
2. _____
3. _____
4. _____
5. _____

③ **Complete each sentence with *This, That, These,* or *Those.***

1. (You are wearing a watch on your wrist.) ___*This*___ is my watch.
2. (Your shoes are across the room near the door.) _____ are my shoes.
3. (You are holding two pens in your hand.) _____ are my pens.
4. (You are in room 210.) _____ is room 210.
5. (You are pointing to a car across the street.) _____ is my car.

4 Complete the conversations. Use *What does he/she look like?* or *What is he/she like?*

1. A: <u>What does he look like?</u>

   B: He's tall and thin.

2. A: _____

   B: She's very friendly.

3. A: _____

   B: She has blond hair.

4. A: _____

   B: He's very easygoing.

5. A: _____

   B: He's bald.

5 Complete each sentence with the opposite of the underlined word.

1. He's not <u>talkative</u>. He's <u>d</u> .   a. boring

2. Don't be <u>stingy</u>. Be ____ .   b. easygoing

3. That movie wasn't <u>interesting</u>. It was ____ . c. relaxed

4. She isn't <u>shy</u>. She's ____ .   d. ~~quiet~~

5. The teacher isn't <u>funny</u>. He's ____ .   e. outgoing

6. On weekends I'm not <u>energetic</u>. I'm ____ .   f. nice

7. She's not <u>mean</u>. She's very ____ .   g. generous

8. My boss isn't very <u>intense</u>. He's pretty ____ . h. serious

6 Complete the conversations. Use *Thank you, No, thank you,* or *Yes, please.*

1. A: Would you like some cookies?   B: <u>No, thank you.</u>   Not right now.

2. A: Would you like a glass of water?   B: _____ That would be nice.

3. A: Those are very nice shoes.   B: _____

4. A: How about some salad?   B: _____ I don't like salad.

5. A: I like your coat.   B: _____

Erika Needs a Job

1 **Answer the questions about the jobs. Circle *True* or *False*.**

Job 1

HELP WANTED
FT Waiter/Waitress
One year experience necessary.
Some evening and
weekend work required.
Must speak 2 languages.
Apply in person.
Moonlight Restaurant. 36 Jane Street.

Job 2

HELP WANTED
PT School Aide
Hours: 10 A.M. to 2 P.M.
Friendly, relaxed classroom.
Interesting coworkers.
No nights or weekends.
Call 404-555-8796.

Job 3

SALES MANAGER NEEDED
Busy store.
Two years experience necessary.
Responsible for 24 salespeople.
Hours: 9:00 to 5:00.
Own transportation necessary.
Fax resume: 404-788-9485.

1. Job 1 does not require experience. True (False)

2. Job 3 requires experience. True False

3. Job 3 is a full time job. True False

4. Job 2 does not require experience. True False

5. You can send a resume to apply for Job 1. True False

6. Job 2 is a full time job. True False

7. Job 3 requires a car. True False

8. You can send a resume to apply for Job 3. True False

2 **Complete each sentence with the correct ending.**

1. I make enough to pay __e__ . a. several software programs

2. But I want to earn ____ . b. phones

3. Tomorrow I will look ____ . c. directions

4. I will read ____ . d. for a job

5. An office assistant has to answer ____ . e. ~~my bills~~

6. An office assistant also has to take ____ . f. messages

7. I get ____ . g. special skills

8. I can also follow ____ . h. the want ads

9. Some jobs require ____ . i. along well with people

10. I am able to use ____ . j. a good salary

3 **Look at the job ads on page 13 of your Student Book. Choose a job that would be good for you. Tell why you think you should apply for the job.**

_____

_____

_____

4 **Rearrange the words to write the correct sentences.**

A: Good morning. (job / the / mechanic's / available / is / still)

(1) _Is the mechanic's job still available?_____

B: Yes, it is.

A: (schedule / work / you / can / me / tell / about / the)

(2) _____

B: (part-time / it's / job / a)

(3) _____

A: (job / required / is / for / the / what)

(4) _____

B: (need / you / experience / years / two

(5) _____

A: (can / apply / how / I)

(6) _____

B: (person / in / apply / you / can / at 79 Main Street)

(7) _____

5 **Complete each sentence with the simple present or present continuous form of the verb in parentheses.**

1. I _____ _buy_ _____ (buy) a newspaper every morning.

2. Then I _____ (read) the help wanted ads.

3. I _____ (look) for a new job now.

4. I _____ (apply) for two or three jobs every week.

5. I _____ (interview) for a job at 3:00 this afternoon.

6. I _____ (type) my resume right now.

7. I always _____ (arrive) early for interviews.

8. I _____ (leave) here at 2:00.

Review

① Bubble the correct answers.

a   b   c

1. _____ apartment do you live in?
   a) Who   b) Which   c) Where   ○ ○ ○

2. We live near the school, and they do, _____.
   a) too   b) so   c) now   ○ ○ ○

3. She reads the help wanted ads _____.
   a) always   b) never   c) once a week   ○ ○ ○

4. _____ are very nice shoes.
   a) Those   b) That   c) This   ○ ○ ○

5. Everyone wants _____ friends.
   a) stingy   b) nice   c) boring   ○ ○ ○

6. We _____ soccer twice a week.
   a) playing   b) are playing   c) play   ○ ○ ○

② Read the advice column. Then answer the question.

Dear Ms. Know It All,

    I want to get a job as an office assistant. I'm very responsible and punctual and I can speak English very well. I'm sure I can handle the phones and the word processing. But I don't have some of the special skills they want—like experience with spreadsheet programs. Also, I only have six months' experience and they want two years. Should I forget about the job? Should I apply and pretend I have the skills? Or should I apply and tell the truth about myself?

—Confused in Chicago

Dear Confused,

    Go for it. Apply for the job, but don't tell them you have only six months' experience. You'll learn a lot the first few weeks on the job. Your coworkers will help you learn what you need to know. You'll be fine!

—Ms. Know It All

Critical Thinking:

What do you think of Ms. Know It All's advice? Do you agree or disagree? On a piece of paper, write your own letter of advice to *Confused in Chicago*.

Love and Marriage

2

Vocabulary

1 **Rearrange the letters to form a word. Fill in the blank with the word.**

1. (derriam)   Jack and I got _____married_____ last June.

2. (dewtia)   We _____ until September to go on vacation together.

3. (dededic)   We _____ to visit California.

4. (citnafsat)   We had a _____ vacation.

5. (welf)   We _____ from New York to Los Angeles.

6. (dedobar)   We _____ the plane in New York at 9:00 and arrived at 2:00 in the afternoon.

7. (rooduot)   First we had coffee at an _____ café.

8. (morcitan)   Later we had dinner in a _____ restaurant.

9. (hemowont)   Later we visited Jack's parents in his _____, San Diego.

10. (detroniucd)   He also _____ me to his three cousins who live there too.

2 **Complete the sentences with the correct word from the box.**

on	got	had	thought	came	returned	reception	felt	communicate	~~told~~

1. Francisco _____told_____ Maria that he loved her.

2. Maria and Fatma _____ in English because they both speak that language.

3. When Sid invited me to visit him, I _____ about it for a couple of days.

4. I went home for lunch at noon, but I _____ back for class at 3:00.

5. The Peterman family went to Paris _____ vacation.

6. The Petermans _____ last Sunday.

7. Celia _____ engaged last summer.

8. She _____ very happy.

9. Everyone _____ a wonderful time at Celia's wedding.

10. The wedding _____ lasted for three hours.

Newlyweds

❶ Complete the sentences. Use the correct past tense form of the verbs from the box.

| stay go decide meet teach talk take eat begin drive read drink be learn |

1. Jane ___went___ to the library yesterday.

2. She _____ her friend, Alice, there.

3. First they _____ about school for a few minutes.

4. Then they _____ magazines.

5. Linda and Tim _____ to go to a café.

6. Tim _____ a cup of coffee.

7. Linda _____ a muffin.

8. They _____ for over two hours.

9. Erik _____ his driving test yesterday.

10. He _____ a little nervous.

11. But he _____ very well.

12. Several students _____ to the computer center.

13. The teacher _____ them a lesson.

14. They _____ a lot about computers.

15. The class _____ at 2:00 and ended at 3:00.

❷ Choose the correct pronunciation of the *-ed* ending.

	/t/	/d/	/id/
1. played	○	●	○
2. rested	○	○	○
3. danced	○	○	○
4. listened	○	○	○
5. watched	○	○	○

	/t/	/d/	/id/
6. married	○	○	○
7. needed	○	○	○
8. cooked	○	○	○
9. attended	○	○	○
10. lasted	○	○	○

3 **Number the lines of each conversation in the correct order.**

1.

____ I danced all night.

_1_ Did you enjoy Mark's wedding?

____ Yes, I did.

____ No wonder you had a good time.

____ Why? What did you do?

2.

____ So that's why you didn't call me.

____ Did you pay all your bills?

____ The telephone company turned off my phone.

____ No. I didn't have enough money.

____ So what happened?

3.

____ Did you go to English class?

____ Oh? I'm glad I stayed home.

____ Did you go to school yesterday?

____ Yes, I did.

____ Yes, and the teacher gave a test.

4.

____ We're having a test and you need it.

____ Did you bring your dictionary today?

____ Don't worry. You can use mine.

____ No, I didn't. Why?

____ Well, I left it on my desk at home.

4 **Choose a topic. Write a conversation about a past event like those in Activity 3.**

A: _____

B: _____

A: _____

B: _____

A: _____

5 **Write the words from the box in the correct spaces on the picture.**

1. _____
2. _____
3. _____
4. _____
5. _____
6. _____
7. _____

Welcome To The Wedding

for Jim and Tina

| newlyweds |
| wedding cake |
| bride |
| maid of honor |
| reception |
| best man |
| groom |

Changes

① Complete the conversations. Add the words *used to, still,* or *anymore* to each line.

1. A: Do you _____still_____ live with your parents?

   B: I _____ live with them, but I don't live with them _____.

2. A: Is it _____ raining?

   B: Yes, it is _____ raining.

3. A: Do you _____ go to school?

   B: No, I don't go to school _____, but I _____ go to school.

4. A: Are you _____ nervous?

   B: No, I'm not nervous _____.

5. A: Does your brother _____ smoke?

   B: No, he _____ smoke, but he doesn't smoke _____.

② Complete the sentences with *use to* or *used to.*

1. A: Did you _____use to_____ watch TV every night?

   B: No, but I _____used to_____ listen to the radio a lot.

2. A: What did you _____ do on Saturday mornings?

   B: I _____ sleep until noon.

3. A: The bus _____ come at 2:00.

   B: I know. I _____ take it every afternoon.

4. A: We _____ live on Continental Avenue.

   B: You did? My uncle _____ live near there.

5. A: When did you _____ get up on weekdays?

   B: I _____ get up at 7:00.

6. A: I didn't _____ like vegetables at all when I was a child.

   B: I didn't either. I _____ give mine to the dog.

3 **Rewrite each sentence. Add the word *still* or *anymore*. If both forms are correct, write the sentence both ways.**

1. I don't have a cat. *I don't have a cat anymore. / I still don't have a cat.*

2. Are you looking for a job? _____

3. Does Rachel study a lot? _____

4. They closed the mall so we don't go there. _____

5. This room doesn't have enough desks. _____

6. Is Tom working as a mechanic? _____

4 **Write about yourself or someone you know. Describe the following:**

1. a healthy thing the person did in the past, but doesn't do now

_____

2. an unhealthy thing the person did in the past, but doesn't do now

_____

3. a healthy thing the person did in the past and continues to do now

_____

4. an unhealthy thing the person did in the past and continues to do now

_____

5 **Complete the sentences to show positive or negative agreement.**

	Speaks Spanish	Likes pizza	Got married	Lived in Boston
Anna	Yes	Yes	No	Yes
Carlos	Yes	No	Yes	No
Bill	No	Yes	Yes	No
Susan	No	No	No	Yes

1. Anna speaks Spanish, and *Carlos does, too.* (Carlos)

Bill doesn't speak Spanish, and *Susan doesn't either / neither does Susan.* (Susan)

2. Susan doesn't like pizza, and _____. (Carlos)

Bill likes pizza, and _____. (Anna)

3. Anna didn't get married, and _____. (Susan)

Carlos got married, and _____. (Bill)

4. Anna lived in Boston, and _____. (Susan)

Carlos didn't live in Boston, and _____. (Bill)

Career Ladders

1 **Complete the lists with jobs from the box.**

carpenter	~~mechanic's helper~~	teller
real estate agency secretary	contractor	assistant service manager
real estate agent	assistant teller	service department manager
real estate sales assistant	loan officer	construction laborer

Entry-level	**Mid-level**	**Upper-level**
mechanic's helper	_____	_____
_____	_____	_____
_____	_____	_____
_____	_____	_____

2 **Rewrite the incorrect questions and answers. Write *correct* if the sentence has no mistakes.**

1. Q: You will be here tomorrow?   _Will you be here tomorrow?_

   A: Yes, I will.   _correct_

2. Q: Will she find a job soon?   _____

   A: No, she not.   _____

3. Q: Will an entry-level position he get?   _____

   A: No, he won't.   _____

4. Q: Will they change jobs soon?   _____

   A: Yes, they'll.   _____

5. Q: You will take just any job?   _____

   A: No, I won't.   _____

6. Q: This will be an interesting job?   _____

   A: No, it won't.   _____

❸ Number the lines of each conversation in the correct order.

1.

____ He's a full-time salesperson.

_1_ What was Joe's last job?

____ If all goes well, he will be a sales manager.

____ He was a part-time salesperson.

____ What does he do now?

____ What is his goal for the future?

2.

____ What does she do now?

____ She was a receptionist.

____ What did Sarah used to do?

____ She hopes to be an office manager.

____ She's a secretary.

____ What will she do in the future?

3.

____ I was a waitress.

____ What was your last job?

____ What do you do now?

____ I'd like to be a restaurant manager.

____ I'm an assistant manager of a restaurant.

____ What would you like to do next?

4.

____ He wants to be a principal.

____ He was a teacher's aide.

____ He's a teacher.

____ What was Mr. Lee's last job?

____ What is his job now?

____ What is his future goal?

❹ Write an interview like the ones in Activity 3. Ask yourself questions. Give true or made-up answers.

Interviewer: _____

You: _____

Interviewer: _____

You: _____

Interviewer: _____

You: _____

❺ Read the conversations and complete the work history section of the applications.

1. A: Tell me a little about your experience.

   B: Well, right now I work at Paula's Pizzeria.

   A: What is your position?

   B: I'm a cook.

   A: When did you start there?

   B: In December 2005.

   A: Why are you leaving?

   B: I need to earn more money.

   EXPERIENCE

   CURRENT JOB: _____

   POSITION: _____

   REASON FOR LEAVING: _____

   DATE: _____

2. A: Where are you working now?

B: I'm a plumber's assistant at Pete's Plumbing.

A: When did you begin working there?

B: In March 2006.

A: Why do you want to leave that job?

B: I'm looking for an opportunity for advancement. I want to get a job as a plumber.

EXPERIENCE

CURRENT JOB: _____

POSITION: _____

REASON FOR LEAVING: _____

DATE: _____

3. A: Tell me a little about your work experience.

B: I'm working at Jerry's Jeans.

A: What do you do?

B: I'm a clothing salesperson. I started in August 2006.

A: Why are you leaving your current job?

B: I'm planning to move to this city. I need a new job.

EXPERIENCE

CURRENT JOB: _____

POSITION: _____

REASON FOR LEAVING: _____

DATE: _____

4. A: So what kind of work experience do you have?

B: Well, right now I work for Cantone Construction.

A: What do you do?

B: I'm a construction laborer.

A: When did you start working for Cantone Construction?

B: In October 2005.

A: Why do you want to leave that job?

B: I want to advance my career. I want to be a carpenter.

EXPERIENCE

CURRENT JOB: _____

POSITION: _____

REASON FOR LEAVING: _____

DATE: _____

Review

1 Bubble the correct answers.

a b c

1. Did you _____ a good time at the wedding?
   a) had   b) have   c) having   ○ ○ ○

2. The party after a wedding is called the _____.
   a) marriage   b) honeymoon   c) reception   ○ ○ ○

3. In many countries, parents _____ their daughter's husbands.
   a) used to choose   b) use to choose   c) used to choosing   ○ ○ ○

4. A long time ago, brides _____ wear white dresses.
   a) don't use to   b) didn't use to   c) didn't used to   ○ ○ ○

5. My grandfather doesn't drive a car _____.
   a) anymore   b) still   c) yet   ○ ○ ○

6. I'm not a manager, and my brother isn't _____.
   a) too   b) neither   c) either   ○ ○ ○

2 Read the story. Then answer the question on a piece of paper.

Modern Weddings

In the United States, the average wedding costs about $25,000—and this doesn't include the wedding rings or the honeymoon. The bride's dress usually costs over $1,000. Gifts for the maid of honor, best man, and others can cost $1,000. Flowers also usually cost about $1,000. If you want photos and a video of your wedding, you'll probably pay at least $2,500, and musicians usually cost at least $500. And then there are the invitations. You can get cheap ones for about $100, but most people get fancy ones and spend at least $500. And, of course, there's transportation. Who doesn't want to leave their wedding in a long black limousine?

Movie stars have some of the most expensive weddings. In order to have a very special private ceremony, they often go to another country. Some of them fly their friends and family halfway around the world and pay for them to stay in fancy hotels for a week. Others rent a boat and have the ceremony somewhere in the middle of the ocean. But evidently a big wedding doesn't always guarantee a good marriage. Just look at the divorce figures for Hollywood couples.

Critical Thinking:

What do you think about the weddings described in this article? Give reasons for your answer. What type of wedding do you prefer? Describe your ideal wedding.

Family Economics

Vocabulary

❶ Complete each sentence with the correct ending.

1. There was a lot of delicious __d__ .
2. Thirteen is my lucky ____.
3. I want to get to know you ____.
4. My sister owes me ____.
5. My favorite party food is barbecued ____.
6. Pizza is my favorite ____.
7. I need to type up ____.
8. We are going to a surprise ____.
9. I will use my credit ____.
10. I'd like some ice cream with my birthday ____.

a. a lot of money
b. food
c. party on Saturday night
d. ~~food at the party~~
e. cake
f. card to buy a birthday gift
g. my resumé this afternoon
h. chicken
i. better
j. number

❷ Choose the correct answers.

1. A *present* is a kind of ____.
   a. dance   b. gift   c. food

2. People put candles on a ____.
   a. cake   b. resume   c. shirt

3. The opposite of *outside the house* is ____.
   a. in front of the house   b. beside the house   c. in the house

4. I ____ take the bus home, but I'm not sure.
   a. will   b. do   c. may

5. We ____ late to class. That is definite.
   a. may be   b. are going to be   c. might be

Plans and Predictions

1 Use the sentences from the box to complete the conversations.

Conversation 1

A: What is your father going to get your mother for her birthday?

B: He's going to get her a toaster.

A: *Are you sure?*

B: Yes, I am. He told me yesterday.

A: _____

B: Why? We need a new toaster.

A: Who wants a toaster as a birthday present? She'll be angry.

B: _____ He's already bought it.

Don't worry.	That's a good idea.
Are you sure?	I hope so.
That's a bad idea.	I hope not.

Conversation 2

A: Paul's going to buy his girlfriend a dog for her birthday.

B: _____

A: Yes, I am. He's buying her a big black dog.

B: _____ I'm sure she'll like it.

A: _____

B: _____ She'll love it.

2 Write a conversation like those in Activity 1. Write about yourself and a friend or family member.

A: _____

B: _____

A: _____

B: _____

A: _____

B: _____

A: _____

3 **Look at each picture and complete the second sentence. Use *will* + *probably* or *be going to*.**

1.

   Alice knows what she wants to do on Saturday morning.

   She *is going to play tennis* with her friends.

2.

   Alice doesn't have definite plans for Sunday afternoon.

   She _____.

3.

   Alice knows what she wants to do on her vacation.

   She _____.

4.

   Alice has already decided what to do on Monday.

   She _____.

5.

   Alice thinks she knows what is happening on Friday night.

   She _____ with Harry Friday night.

6.

   Alice knows what she wants to do tonight.

   She _____.

4 **Circle the correct word in each sentence.**

1. I got (**a** / **an** / (**some**)) junk mail this morning.
2. I used (**a** / **an** / **some**) credit card to buy the gift.
3. I ate (**a** / **an** / **some**) apple for lunch.
4. Did you buy your girlfriend (**a** / **an** / **some**) necklace for her birthday?
5. I need (**a** / **an** / **some**) new furniture for my apartment.
6. There is (**a** / **an** / **some**) old tree outside our house.
7. I need to get (**a** / **an** / **some**) cash from the cash machine.
8. Can I borrow (**a** / **an** / **some**) dollar from you?
9. I'd like (**a** / **an** / **some**) sugar in my coffee.
10. I found (**a** / **an** / **some**) money on the ground.

Money

❶ Match each item with the correct definition.

1. regular hours __e__
2. FICA tax ____
3. net ____
4. OT ____
5. gross ____
6. $7.50 an hour ____
7. federal tax ____
8. NY tax ____

a. state tax
b. U.S. government taxes
c. your pay before taxes are taken out
d. your pay after taxes are taken out
e. ~~35 or 40 hours a week~~
f. social security tax
g. overtime
h. rate of pay

❷ Answer the questions about the pay stubs.

PAYMENT RECEIPT

EMPLOYEE:
Joseph Graf
ID:
569988
DATE: June 30

REGULAR HOURS: 80
RATE: $9.00/hour
OT hours: 10
OT rate: $12.00/hour
GROSS PAY: **$840.00**
FICA: $25.70
Fed: $86.70
State: $16.10
Med Ins: $36.20
NET PAY: $635.30

PAYMENT RECEIPT

EMPLOYEE:
Carol Kissena
ID:
244865
DATE: April 30

REGULAR HOURS: 160
RATE: $10.00/hour
OT hours: 2
OT rate: $15.00/hour
GROSS PAY: **$1,630.00**
FICA: $38.90
Fed: $167.30
State: $34.50
Med Ins: Provided by employer
NET PAY: $1,389.30

1. Joseph's employer pays for his medical insurance.   True   ~~False~~
2. Joseph earns $9.00 an hour for overtime.   True   False
3. Carol is paid once a week.   True   False
4. Carol pays $38.90 in social security taxes.   True   False
5. Carol earns $15.00 an hour for her regular hours.   True   False
6. Joseph's gross pay is correct.   True   False
7. Joseph's net pay is correct.   True   False
8. Carol's net pay is correct.   True   False

3 **Complete the lists with words from the box. Use each word once.**

~~fast food~~	groceries	snacks	savings	clothing	car payment
restaurant meals	rent	water	car insurance	cell phone	
electricity	gas	parking fees	buses	entertainment	

1. **Food costs**

   fast food _____

   _____

   _____

   _____

2. **Apartment expenses**

   _____

   _____

   _____

   _____

3. **Transportation costs**

   _____

   _____

   _____

4. **Other expenses**

   _____

   _____

   _____

4 **Complete the sentences with the correct tense of the verb in parentheses.**

1. If it _____*rains*_____ (rain) tomorrow, we _____*won't go*_____ (not go) to the beach.

2. I _____ (go) to the movies tonight if I _____ (not be) tired.

3. She _____ (be) disappointed if we _____ (not go) to the movies.

4. If we _____ (win) the game, everyone _____ (be) happy.

5. He _____ (not go) out dancing if he _____ (have) a test the next day.

5 **Write three sentences about yourself. Use *if* clauses like those in Activity 4.**

_____

_____

_____

⑥ Circle the correct answers about the coupons.

1. What is the sale price for Riley's Tomato Soup?   a.(ⓢ.33)   b. $.39
2. When does the Riley's soup coupon expire?   a. January 6   b. June 1
3. How much would you pay for a new $600 bicycle on March 8?   a. $480   b. $600
4. How much would you pay for a new $400 bicycle on March 12?   a. $400   b. $320
5. How much would you pay for a $50 bike lock on March 16?   a. $40   b. $50
6. How much would you pay for two $50 chairs on sale?   a. $90   b. $80
7. How much would you pay for a $100 dining table on April 5?   a. $100   b. $90
8. How much would you pay for a $1,000 sofa on April 12?   a. $900   b. $1,000

⑦ Complete each sentence with a word or phrase from the box.

| credit card | ~~store charge card~~ | debit card | annual fee |
| loan | interest | overdraft penalty | late fee |

1. Wal-Mart™ has its own _store charge card._____

2. Money you borrow from a bank is called a _____.

3. You do not pay interest when you use a _____.

4. You usually pay over 14 percent interest when you use a _____.

5. Once a year you pay an _____ on some credit cards.

6. If you don't pay your bill on time, you may have to pay a _____.

7. Money you pay for borrowing money is called _____.

8. If you write a $500 check but have only $300 in the bank,
   you will pay an _____.

Hopes and Dreams

❶ Circle the correct verb or infinitive in each sentence.

1. I intend (**go** / **to go**) to the movies tonight.
2. Do you know how (**drive** / **to drive**) a car?
3. She will not (**arrive** / **to arrive**) on time.
4. We plan (**have** / **to have**) three children.
5. He doesn't (**have** / **to have**) a job right now.
6. They don't expect (**buy** / **to buy**) a new car this year.
7. Did you learn how (**type** / **to type**) yet?
8. Did you (**meet** / **to meet**) your husband at a party?
9. Do they plan (**pay** / **to pay**) over $5,000 for the car?
10. Did you decide (**go** / **to go**) to the party tomorrow night?

❷ Number the lines of each conversation in the correct order.

1.

____ Then I want to become a real estate agent.

____ And then?

_1_ What are your plans for the future?

____ After I take the course, I hope to get a real estate license.

____ And after you take the course?

____ First I plan to take a course in selling real estate.

2.

____ And then?

____ And when you find the house you want?

____ How do you plan to buy a house?

____ Then I'll look until I find the right place.

____ I'll put a down payment on the house and buy it.

____ First I'll save up a lot of money.

3.

____ Then I'll teach him how to read.

____ How do you plan to prepare your son for kindergarten?

____ Then he'll probably be ready for school.

____ First I want to teach him the letters of the alphabet.

____ Then what?

____ And after he learns to read?

4.

____ And after you practice driving?

____ How will you get your driver's license?

____ Then I'll practice driving for a few weeks.

____ Well, first I'll get a learner's permit.

____ And then what?

____ Then I'll take my road test and hope to pass it.

❸ Complete each sentence with the word in parentheses. Write it in the correct blank. Put an *X* in the other blank.

1. (after) *After*_____ I get my consumer loan, _____*X*_____ I am going to buy a lot of new furniture.

2. (when) _____ I plan to drive to work _____ I get my new car.

3. (after) _____ Lena hopes to get a good job _____ she finishes college.

4. (as soon as) _____ Jim finishes his resume, _____ he plans to send it out.

5. (before) _____ I plan to study a lot _____ I take the test.

6. (if) _____ I fail the test, _____ I intend to take it again.

7. (when) _____ Sarah arrives home, _____ we will have dinner.

8. (if) _____ David gets home first, _____ he will start cooking dinner.

9. (before) _____ I buy a house, _____ I intend to save up at least $5,000.

10. (after) _____ I expect to have children _____ I get married.

❹ Use the words in parentheses to write a sentence about future plans.

1. (Tina / finish her resume / this weekend)   Use the present continuous.

   *Tina is going to finish her resume this weekend.*_____

2. (We / visit our parents / tomorrow)   Use *going to*.

   _____

3. (I / use my credit card / to buy furniture)   Use the present continuous.

   _____

4. (John / make a cake tonight)   Use *plan to*.

   _____

5. (It / rain tomorrow)   Use the present continuous.

   _____

6. (Robert / apply for a credit card next month)   Use the present continuous.

   _____

1 Bubble the correct answers.

a b c

1. Harold expects _____ home by 5:00.

   a) will get   b) getting   c) to get   ○ ○ ○

2. I _____ the TV as soon as I get home.

   a) am turning on   b) turn on   c) turning on   ○ ○ ○

3. You sometimes pay _____ once a year if you have a credit card.

   a) an overdraft penalty b) a late fee   c) an annual fee   ○ ○ ○

4. Your _____ is always more than your net pay.

   a) gross pay   b) FICA   c) overtime pay   ○ ○ ○

5. You _____ probably finish the test before 2:00.

   a) are going to   b) will   c) plan   ○ ○ ○

6. They're _____ at 3:00 this afternoon.

   a) leave   b) will leave   c) leaving   ○ ○ ○

2 Read the story. Fill in the blank at the end of each sentence with *F* for *fact* and *O* for *opinion*. Then answer the questions.

The Best Way to Buy Your First Home

I think the best way to buy your first home is to buy a two-family house. (1) __O__ Last Sunday's newspaper listed 18 of these houses in the real estate section. (2) _____ The cheapest one was only $175,000. (3) _____ That sounds like a lot, but it really isn't. (4) _____ Look at it this way. If you make a down payment of $20,000 the principal you are paying off is only $155,000. (5) _____ If you get a 6.5 percent mortgage, the monthly payments are only $979. (6) _____ With another family paying $600 rent for their half, your monthly rent is only $379! (7) _____ That's really cheap! (8) _____ I think everybody should buy a two-family house. (9) _____ The rent from the other half of the house helps pay off the mortgage. (10) _____

Critical Thinking:

What do you think of the suggestions in the story? Would you do this? On a piece of paper, write why or why not.

The Community

Chapter 4

Vocabulary

❶ Fill in the blanks. Use the words from the box.

library	clinic	employment agency	police station	fire station
~~supermarket~~	café	health club	park	
movie theater	video store	laundromat	adult school	

My neighborhood is a great place to be on the weekend when I'm not working. If I'm hungry, I can pick up groceries at the (1) _____supermarket_____. There are also a lot of things to do to relax. I can get a book from the (2) _____ or take a walk in the (3) _____. I can rent a DVD at the (4) _____ or go see a movie at the (5) _____ with my friends. After the movie, we can have a cup of coffee at a (6) _____. On weekends I can exercise at the local (7) _____. The only thing I have to do that isn't relaxing is my laundry. I have to spend some time at the (8) _____ every weekend.

But my neighborhood isn't all about relaxing. There are also serious things happening. There's an (9) _____ where people study English and take job preparation courses. There's also an (10) _____ to help them find jobs when they finish school. If I don't feel well, I can see a doctor right away at the (11) _____. There are always officers at the (12) _____ helping keep the community safe. And if there is a fire, the people at the (13) _____ will take care of the problem.

❷ Which of the places from Activity 1 do you have in your neighborhood?

_____

Give the exact names of several of the places in your neighborhood and briefly describe each one.

_____

_____

_____

_____

_____

❶ Complete the lists with words from the box. Use each word once.

Eli Avenue Hospital	job center	bus information	job training
community college information	train information	emergency room	fire
police	new K-12 students	community clinic	taxi service
~~traffic information~~	immunizations	library information	adult school

1. Transportation

traffic information

_____

_____

_____

2. Education

_____

_____

_____

_____

3. Government

_____

_____

_____

_____

4. Health

_____

_____

_____

_____

❷ Look at the pictures and complete the conversations. Use your own ideas.

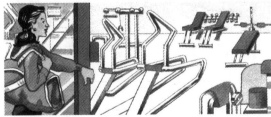

1.

A: Where are you going?

B: _____

A: Why are you going there?

B: _____

A: That's a great idea!

2.

A: Where are you going?

B: _____

A: Why are you going there?

B: _____

A: That's a good reason.

3 **Cross out the incorrect word or words. Then write the correct word or words in the blank.**

1. They went to the bank to ~~opened~~ an account.   *open*

2. I went to the clinic in order get an immunization.   _____

3. She is going to the store order to buy some bread.   _____

4. We went to the post office buy stamps.   _____

5. We are using the dictionary in order to learning new words.   _____

6. I went to the supermarket for buy some food.   _____

7. I studied a lot in order to passed the test.   _____

8. I called the police in order for report an emergency.   _____

4 **Read the article. Take notes about the most important information.**

> **Recycling Schedule**
> **Winston, Maine**
>
> We are happy to announce Winston's new recycling program will begin on June 1. As of that day, homes and businesses in the community will be able to recycle all forms of paper, as well as plastics and most types of metal. Newspapers and other waste paper will be picked up at homes and offices on the first Friday of each month. Please place the materials in clean containers and put the containers in your driveway before 7:00 A.M.
>
> The Recycling Center on Main Street will be open for you to drop off plastic and metal items Monday and Wednesday from noon to 7:00 P.M. Regular household trash will be picked up on Thursday and Saturday afternoons. Please place your trash containers in your driveway before 10:00 A.M.

_____

_____

_____

_____

_____

_____

_____

_____

Working Together

Lesson 2

① Circle *True* or *False*.

1. Using an ATM at night is a good idea.	True	**False**
2. Carrying around a lot of money is a bad idea.	True	False
3. Waiting at a bus stop at night can be dangerous.	True	False
4. Avoiding walking alone at night is a good idea.	True	False
5. Going places where people use drugs is a bad idea.	True	False
6. Leaving your windows open at night is a good idea.	True	False

② Circle the correct word or words in each sentence.

1. I avoid (**to walk** / **walking**) home alone at night.
2. Most teenage boys (**enjoy** / **like**) to drive.
3. We (**hate** / **dislike**) to clean the garage.
4. He talked about (**to go** / **going**) to college next year.
5. We started (**to walk** / **walk**) home at 3:00.
6. My father quit (**to smoke** / **smoking**) last year.
7. He (**continued** / **considered**) to exercise every day.
8. Did they discuss (**to get** / **getting**) married?

③ Complete each sentence with the correct word from the box.

don't mind consider discuss quit ~~avoid~~ enjoy

1. I hate doing the dishes so I always ____*avoid*____ that job.
2. Some people hate washing the car. I don't love it, but I _____ it too much.
3. I want to _____ smoking. I think it's bad for my health.
4. Have you thought about moving to California? Maybe you should _____ it.
5. Let's talk some more. We need to _____ this completely.
6. I _____ listening to music. It really relaxes me.

Lesson 2   Working Together   31

④ Circle the correct answers.

1. Please don't ask me to take out the trash. I _____ doing that.

   a. enjoy   b. don't mind   c. dislike

2. I love to swim. I _____ living near the ocean.

   a. enjoy   b. don't mind   c. dislike

3. I _____ other people smoking if they do it outside.

   a. enjoy   b. don't mind   c. dislike

4. I _____ living in an apartment because I always have noisy neighbors.

   a. enjoy   b. don't mind   c. dislike

5. I eat in restaurants as often as I can. I _____ having someone else make my food.

   a. enjoy   b. don't mind   c. dislike

6. Cold soup isn't my favorite meal, but I _____ it too much.

   a. enjoy   b. don't mind   c. dislike

7. I _____ big, noisy parties. They make me nervous. But I love a small quiet party.

   a. enjoy   b. don't mind   c. dislike

8. I _____ if the windows are open or closed. I'm happy either way.

   a. enjoy   b. don't mind   c. dislike

⑤ Cross out the incorrect verb. Then write the correct verb in the blank. Use the words from the box.

practice	wait	take	~~fill out~~	show	study	pass	pay

1. I need to ~~study~~ my driver's license application.   _____*fill out*_____

2. I will pass driving for several weeks before I take the driving test. _____

3. You need to fill out identification to apply for a driver's license. _____

4. You may have to take in line for a long time. _____

5. I hope I study the written test the first time. _____

6. I will wear my glasses when I show the vision test. _____

7. I need to read a lot for the written test. _____

8. You have to pass a $20 fee for your license. _____

1 **Complete each sentence with the correct ending.**

1. You are absolutely __e__ .
2. I want to find a job in the local ____ .
3. She needs to learn to speak more ____ .
4. I think you should talk to a job ____ .
5. If you don't know the alphabet, you won't be good at ____ .
6. The record of the checks you write should be ____ .
7. Becoming a doctor requires very ____ .
8. If you're considering changing jobs, you should visit the employment ____ .
9. She plans to become a manager, but right now she an administrative ____ .
10. I am looking for a higher-paying ____ .

a. assistant
b. filing
c. position
d. fluently
e. ~~wonderful~~
f. agency
g. specialized training
h. area
i. accurate
j. counselor

2 **Circle the correct word or words in each sentence.**

1. He is a ((quick) / quickly) learner.
2. She drives very (good / well).
3. He is a (hard / hardly) worker.
4. How (fluent / fluently) do you speak English?
5. My father is a (slow / slowly) driver.
6. I complete my assignments (careful / carefully).
7. That was a very (easy / easily) test.
8. If you walk (fast / fastly), you won't be late to class.
9. She is a very (good / well) cook.
10. Please add up the numbers again. I don't think your answer is (accurate / accurately).

3 Cross out the incorrect word or words. Then write the correct word or words in the blank. Write *correct* if the sentence has no mistakes.

1. I think the red dress is ~~more pretty~~ than the blue one.   _____prettier_____

2. Sally is thinner than her sister.   _____

3. The weather today is more hot than it was yesterday.   _____

4. This room is more big than our old classroom.   _____

5. I am happyer on Fridays than on Mondays.   _____

6. "Thank you" is politer than "thanks."   _____

7. I live more far from school than you do.   _____

8. I feel more well today than I did yesterday.   _____

4 Complete the conversations. Use the correct form of the underlined adjective or adverb.

1. A: Does Susan paint <u>carefully</u>?

   B: No, she's not a very _____careful_____ painter.

2. A: Ellen paints more <u>carefully</u>, right?

   B: Yes. Ellen is a _____ painter.

3. A: And Susan's work isn't very <u>good</u>.

   B: Right. Ellen is a _____ painter.

4. A: But Ellen doesn't work very <u>fast</u>, does she?

   B: No, she doesn't. Susan is a _____ painter.

1. A: Is Jeff a <u>quick</u> learner?

   B: Yes, he learns very _____.

2. A: Is he a <u>hard</u> worker?

   B: Yes, he works _____.

3. A: Is he fast or <u>slow</u>?

   B: He works _____.

4. A: He works <u>carefully</u>, doesn't he?

   B: Yes, he's the _____ worker I know.

5 Read the help wanted ads. Compare the jobs using the words in parentheses.

Job 1

HELP WANTED
TAXI DRIVER
60+ hrs/wk, $9/hr., flexible hours.
Some weekend work necessary.
Start this week.
Some medical paid.

Job 2

HELP WANTED
Teacher's Aide
Set hours: M-F 8-4.
40 hrs/wk. $6/hr. No OT.
Start in 4 weeks.
Must speak good English.
Full medical paid.

1. (have, high salary)   Job 1 has a higher salary.

2. (start, soon)   _____

3. (have, long hours)   _____

4. (have, good benefits)   _____

5. (require, fluency in English)   _____

6. (have, flexible schedule)   _____

6 Guess what the underlined words mean by looking at the sentences around them. Circle the correct meaning.

1. She was making a cup of tea. She used <u>boiling</u> water.

   a. cold   b. fresh   c. very hot

2. Their apartment has four bedrooms. It is really <u>spacious</u>.

   a. large   b. expensive   c. convenient

3. Thelma exercises every day. She is very <u>athletic</u>.

   a. busy   b. strong   c. tired

4. This math problem is really difficult. Can you help me find the <u>solution</u>?

   a. answer   b. word   c. beginning

5. I can't read some of the words on the directory. Can you help me <u>interpret</u> what it says?

   a. write   b. ask   c. understand

Review

❶ Bubble the correct answers.

a   b   c

1. I need to study more _____ better grades.
   a) get   b) in order get   c) in order to get   ○ ○ ○

2. A woman ought to get pre-natal care at _____.
   a) an emergency room   b) a clinic   c) a library   ○ ○ ○

3. Sue doesn't mind _____ at home every night.
   a) to eat   b) eating   c) eat   ○ ○ ○

4. Math is _____ than science for me.
   a) harder   b) more hard   c) more harder   ○ ○ ○

5. The local supermarket is _____ than the one downtown.
   a) more convenient   b) convenient   c) more conveniently   ○ ○ ○

6. I want to be healthy so I _____ smoking.
   a) consider   b) enjoy   c) avoid   ○ ○ ○

❷ Read the advice column. Then answer the questions.

Dear Ms. Know It All,

I live in a neighborhood that doesn't always seem safe at night. Every couple weeks someone has their wallet or purse taken while walking down the street. My family tells me that I just have to accept it and not go out after dark. But what kind of life is that? I work all day and I need to see people at night. I'm pretty strong and I can run fast. I think I'll be OK. What do you think?

—**Not Really Scared**

Dear Not Really Scared,

I think you are partly right. You do need to get out of the house, but I don't think being strong and running fast are going to keep you safe. But there are some things you can do to help protect yourself. Always go out with at least one other person. Don't wear fancy jewelry or clothes and keep your purse or wallet out of sight. Only walk on well-lighted streets. Keep your head up and walk quickly and confidently. This will help keep possible attackers from choosing you as a victim. Good luck!

—**Ms. Know It All**

Critical Thinking:

What do you think of Ms. Know It All's advice. Do you agree or disagree? On a piece of paper, write your own letter of advice to *Not Really Scared*.

People and Places

Chapter 5

Vocabulary

1 Label the four cities on the map.

Las Vegas
Chicago
New York City
San Francisco

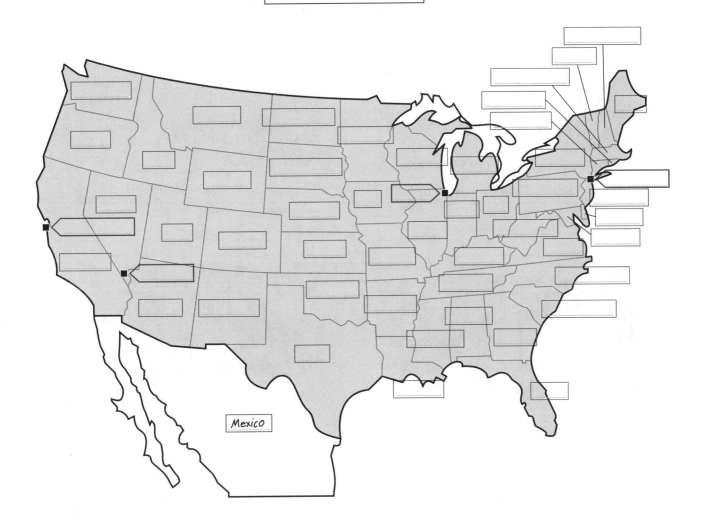

Mexico

2 Write on the map the names of other cities or places you have visited or know about. See how many state names you can fill in.

Have You Ever . . . ?

1 **Look at the pictures. Then complete the conversations with the correct present perfect and past tense forms of the verbs in parentheses.**

1.

A: Have you ever __visited Texas__? (visit)

B: Yes, __I have__ .

A: Really? What did you do there?

B: I __went waterskiing__ . (go water skiing)

A: I __have visited__ Texas several times, too. (visit)

2.

A: Have you ever _____? (fill out)

B: No, _____.

A: Really? Have you ever _____? (have a job)

B: Yes, _____. Have you ever _____? (work)

A: Yes, _____.

3.

A: Have you ever _____? (be to)

B: Yes, _____.

A: What did you do there?

B: We _____ in the mountains. (go hiking)

A: Sounds like fun.

4.

A: Have you ever _____? (change)

B: Yes, _____.

A: Really. When did you do that?

B: I _____ last weekend. (change one)

A: That's interesting!

5.

A: Have you ever _____ (use)

B: Yes, _____.

A: Where did you use it?

B: I _____ it at work. (use) Have you ever _____ one? (use)

A: No, _____.

6.

A: Have you _____. (stop)

B: Yes, _____.

A: When did you stop?

B: I _____ my last cigarette a month ago. (have)

A: Have you _____ to start again? (want)

B: Yes, _____. But I have _____ good. (be)

2 Circle the correct word in each sentence.

1. Classes have (**began** /(**begun**)) for the year.
2. Have you (**seen** / **saw**) the new movie yet?
3. Ms. Johnson has (**teached** / **taught**) English for over ten years.
4. My brother has (**taken** / **took**) a lot of pictures of his baby.
5. What have you (**did** / **done**) with your hair?
6. We have (**gone** / **went**) to the library three times this week.
7. Have you (**red** / **read**) the homework assignment yet?
8. She has (**came** / **come**) to class late every day this week.
9. The weather has (**was** / **been**) hot all week long.
10. Have you (**gotten** / **get**) any mail lately?
11. How much money has she (**gave** / **given**) to the children?
12. Have you (**found** / **find**) the answer to your question yet?

3 Rewrite these past tense sentences in the present perfect tense.

1. I ate too much.
   I have eaten too much.

2. She cut her hair twice this month.
   _____

3. I drove David's new car.
   _____

4. They brought their lunches to the office all week.
   _____

5. Carlos wore the same red shirt every day this week.
   _____

6. I knew a lot of people from Vietnam.
   _____

1 **Complete the conversations. Use the past tense or the past perfect tense of the verb in parentheses.**

Conversation 1

A: _____Has_____ Ali ever __ridden__ a horse?   (ride)

B: Yes, he has.

A: How many times ___has he done it___?   (do it)

B: _He has done it many times._____   (do it / many times)

A: ___Did__ he ever __fall_? (fall)

B: No, he didn't.

Conversation 2

A: _____ you ever _____?   (drive a truck)

B: No, I haven't.

A: _____ you ever _____ to do it?   (want)

B: Yes, I did.

A: Why _____ you _____ it?   (do)

B: I have always been too scared.

Conversation 3

A: When _____ your mother _____ playing tennis?   (start)

B: When she was 13 years old.

A: How long _____?   (play)

B: She's played for over 25 years.

A: _____ you ever _____ against her?   (play)

B: No, I haven't.

A: Why not?

B: I _____ enough yet.   (not practice)

2 Write the full form of the underlined contractions.

1. <u>They've</u> lived in Chicago for ten years.   *They have*

2. <u>They're</u> going to visit friends in New York next week.   _____

3. <u>He's</u> thinking about buying a car.   _____

4. <u>He's</u> read the car advertisements in the newspaper.   _____

5. <u>She's</u> already bought a new car.   _____

6. <u>It's</u> rained every day this week.   _____

7. <u>It's</u> not a good time to go biking.   _____

8. <u>We're</u> planning to go to the movies tonight.   _____

9. <u>We've</u> bought our tickets already.   _____

10. <u>I've</u> read several stories about the movie.   _____

3 Use the present perfect to describe three situations in your life. Use contractions.

_____

_____

_____

4 Complete the sentences. Use superlatives to describe each city.

	Restaurants	People	Stores	Views
Smallville	very good	not friendly	cheap	pretty
Denville	bad	very friendly	expensive	very pretty
Bushville	very bad	friendly	very expensive	ugly

1. Smallville has _____*the best*_____ restaurants.

2. Bushville has _____ restaurants.

3. Denville has _____ people.

4. Bushville has _____ stores.

5. Smallville has _____ stores.

6. Denville has _____ views.

Erika's Job Interview

1 Read the paragraph. Then complete the timeline.

In January, 1997, I moved to the United States. Two months later, I started English classes. I studied hard because I wanted to get a good job. In June, 1998, I got my first job. I was a dishwasher at a restaurant. I continued to study English. Three months later, I became a waiter. The pay for that job was much better. In February, 1999, I started studying business at the community college. In October of that year, I became night manager of the restaurant.

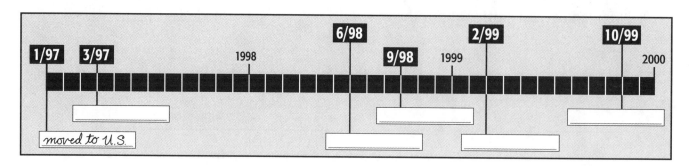

2 Cross out the incorrect word. Then write the correct word in the blank.

1. We have been in class ~~for~~ 8:00. _since_

2. Lisa has known Pablo in 2001. _____

3. They have been in class together since two years. _____

4. Lisa has had the same job from 2002. _____

5. Pablo has been a mechanic since several years. _____

6. Lisa's family has lived in the United States for 2000. _____

7. Her parents have been married in 1980. _____

8. They have lived in the same house in ten years. _____

9. Lisa's mother has had two more children when they moved here. _____

10. She hasn't had a job since 12 years. _____

3 **Scan the story. Underline things people should *wear* and things people should *do* at a job interview. Then write them in the correct column.**

Interview Tips

What do you need to remember when you go for a job interview? First of all, it's important to look right. It's best to choose dark-colored business clothes. Street clothes make it look like you're ready to play, not work. And never wear sneakers. Black shoes are more appropriate for an interview. And don't wear a hat. Most people look less serious when they are wearing a hat. Be sure to arrive early. There's nothing worse than keeping the interviewer waiting. Look the interviewer in the eyes. You may feel nervous, but that will go away soon. And don't forget to say "thank you" at the end of the interview. That always makes a good impression.

Wear   **Do**

_____   _____

_____   _____

_____   _____

_____   _____

4 **Circle the best answers.**

1. Peter is a self-starter. He _____.

   a. always does his best   b. can work alone   c. likes working with people

2. Jack is very reliable. He doesn't _____.

   a. work alone   b. lie or steal   c. work fast

3. Carol is energetic. She _____.

   a. always works slowly   b. is always active   c. always keep her promises

4. Jim is good with people. He _____.

   a. is friendly   b. is honest   c. is always on time

5. Ali is really patient. He _____.

   a. works very fast   b. always does his best   c. doesn't get upset

6. George is a flexible worker. He _____.

   a. is always on time   b. likes working alone   c. doesn't mind changing plans

5 Write the answers to the questions. Use complete sentences with *for* or *since*. Use the information in parentheses.

A: How long have you been in this country?   (2000)

B: *I've been in this country since 2000.*

A: How long have you been a waitress?   (two years)

B: _____

A: How long have you studied English?   (2002)

B: _____

A: How long have you worked at Irene's?   (2004)

B: _____

A: And how long have you lived in Miami?   (2001)

B: _____

6 Prepare for your own job interview. Write some questions and answers about yourself like those in Activity 5.

A: _____

B: _____

A: _____

B: _____

A: _____

B: _____

7 Number the lines of the thank-you note in the correct order.

____ I enjoyed meeting you, and I think I would be good at the job.

____ Sincerely,

____ I look forward to hearing from you.

_1_ Thank you for taking the time to interview me.

____ As I said at the interview, I have been an office assistant for three years.

____ If you need any more information, please don't hesitate to call.

Review

1 Bubble the correct answers.

a b c

1. He's a hard worker. He _____.
   a) does the best he can   b) likes people   c) doesn't get upset easily   ○ ○ ○

2. She has known Jim _____ 1995.
   a) for   b) since   c) from   ○ ○ ○

3. That is the _____ building in the city.
   a) most tall   b) most pretty   c) most beautiful   ○ ○ ○

4. I _____ that movie several times.
   a) have see   b) have saw   c) have seen   ○ ○ ○

5. Have you _____ your homework yet?
   a) begin   b) began   c) begun   ○ ○ ○

6. I _____ in California when I was a teenager.
   a) lived   b) have lived   c) living   ○ ○ ○

2 Study the chart and answer the questions.

Climate and Sports

The U.S. has a wide variety of climates. This means that some cities are great places to ski, while others never have skiing. Some places have perfect beach weather all year round, while others are always cool or cold.

	Annual snowfall in inches	Average January temperature (F)	Average July temperature (F)
Burlington, VT	79.0	18°	71°
Houston, TX	0.4	52°	84°
Los Angeles, CA	0	57°	70°
Tucson, AZ	1.2	52°	87°
Minneapolis, MN	50	13°	73°

1. Which city gets the most snow in January? _____

2. In which cities could you ice skate in January? _____

3. Which city has the highest average summer temperature? _____

4. Which city gets the least snow? _____

5. Which city has the biggest difference between summer and winter temperatures? _____

Vocabulary

1 **Complete each sentence with the correct ending.**

1. Apartments, townhouses, and condos are types of __c__.
2. An apartment complex contains ____.
3. A duplex is an apartment on ____.
4. A place where you pay for one day at a time is a ____.
5. The family in the house next to your house lives ____.
6. A house on wheels is a ____.
7. If you don't own your apartment you pay ____.
8. An apartment you buy is called a ____.
9. Money you pay the bank for your home is called your ____.
10. The people who live together in a home are a ____.

a. mortgage
b. condo
c. ~~housing~~
d. mobile home
e. several buildings
f. next door
g. household
h. hotel
i. two floors
j. rent

2 **Look at the pictures. Circle the correct answers for each.**

1.

This is an example of (**a hotel / a townhouse / a mobile home / an apartment / a home**).

2.

This is an example of (**a condo / housing / a mobile home / an apartment complex**).

3.

This is an example of (**a duplex / a townhouse / a single family home / a household**).

4.

This is an example of (**a townhouse / a hotel / a home / a condo**).

Homes

1 **Complete the conversations with information from the chart.**

	Present home	**Past homes**	**When**
Roger	apartment, 3 months	Atlanta, GA—mobile home	2003–this year
		Miami, FL—condo	1996–2003
Laura	condo, 1 year	Boston, MA—apartment	2002–this year
		Chicago, IL— townhouse	1996–2002
Karen	townhouse, 2 years	Chicago, IL—apartment	2000–this year
		Akron, OH—ranch house	1998–2000
		San Francisco, CA—apartment	1995-1998
David	ranch house, 5 years	Buffalo, NY—ranch house	2004–this year
		Teaneck, NJ—condo	1992–2004

1.

A: **Roger,** what kind of housing do you live in now?

B: I live in _an apartment._

A: How long have you lived there?

B: _I've lived there for three months._

A: How many different places have you lived since 1996?

B: _____

A: Have you ever lived in a townhouse?

B: _____

2.

A: **Laura,** what kind of housing do you live in now?

B: I live in _____

A: How long have you lived there?

B: _____

A: How many different places have you lived since 1996?

B: _____

A: Have you ever lived in an apartment?

B: _____

3.

A: **Karen,** what kind of housing do you live in now?

B: I live in _____

A: How long have you lived there?

B: _____

A: How many different places have you lived since 1995?

B: _____

A: Have you ever lived in a condo?

B: _____

4.

A: **David,** what kind of housing do you live in now?

B: I live in _____

A: How long have you lived there?

B: _____

A: How many different places have you lived since 1992?

B: _____

A: Have you ever lived in a condo?

B: _____

② Tell about your own housing situation. Use the conversations in Activity 1 as examples.

_____

_____

③ Answer the questions about the ads.

Apartment 1

1. Apartment 1 allows dogs and cats. (True) False
2. The rent on apartment 1 is $700 a month. True False
3. Apartment 1 has a new bathroom. True False
4. The security deposit on Apartment 2 is $350. True False
5. Apartment 1 is on two floors. True False
6. Apartment 2 has small rooms. True False
7. Apartment 2 is in a bad neighborhood. True False
8. Apartment 2 has a bright living room. True False

Apartment 1

FOR RENT
Rome Avenue Special!
1 BR duplex. 800 sq ft.
Built in 1990. Fireplace in LR.
On busy street.
Bus stop on corner.
New kit/bath. Pets OK.
$900 MO + $450 sec.
Call 718-555-3948

Apartment 2

For Rent
Atom Street Space
1 BR apt. Very large rooms.
800 sq ft. Built in 1990.
Four blocks to bus.
Very safe neighborhood.
Sunny LR. No pets.
$700 MO + $350 sec.
Call 718-555-3939

④ Compare Apartment 1 and Apartment 2 using *as . . . as . . .* comparisons.

1. Apartment 1 _____isn't as bright as_____ Apartment 2. (bright)

2. Apartment 2 _____ Apartment 1. (big)

3. Transportation to Apartment 2 _____ as transportation to Apartment 1. (convenient)

4. The security deposit on Apartment 2 _____ the deposit on Apartment 1. (large)

5. Apartment 1 _____ Apartment 2. (old)

5 Circle the correct answers.

1. Q: How many times have you been to the library?

   A: I've been there (**since 2:00** / **twice**).

2. Q: How long have you come to this class?

   A: I've come here (**for ten times** / **for ten weeks**).

3. Q: How long have you known Susan?

   A: I've known her (**since 1998** / **since three times**).

4. Q: How many times have you moved this year?

   A: I've moved (**once** / **since April**).

5. Q: How long has your family lived in a house?

   A: We've lived here (**for two years** / **two times**).

6 Write sentences using the present perfect. Use the words in parentheses.

1. (Tina / not / see /Joe / recently)   _Tina hasn't seen Joe recently._

2. (I / never/ visit / Paris)   _____

3. (we / never / live in / condo)   _____

4. (Tom / not / study / in a long time)   _____

5. (They / not / see a movie / lately)   _____

6. (You / never / call / me)   _____

7. (I / not / eat pizza / recently)   _____

8. (It / never / snow / in Miami)   _____

7 Write three sentences about people you have or haven't talked to. Use the words *recently, lately, in a long time,* or *never.*

_____

_____

_____

_____

Bills

1 **Complete the lists with words from the box. Use each word once.**

telephone bill	trash removal	car insurance	rent
gas bill	~~mortgage payment~~	car payment	taxi costs
Internet access	homeowner's insurance	electricity bill	bus fare

1. Housing expenses

mortgage payment

_____

_____

_____

2. Utility expenses

_____

_____

_____

_____

3. Transportation expenses

_____

_____

_____

_____

2 **Think about ways you could save money on your housing, utility, or transportation expenses. Write four suggestions to yourself.**

1. _____

2. _____

3. _____

4. _____

3 **Cross out the word that is used incorrectly. Then rewrite the sentence correctly. If the sentence has no mistakes, write *correct* on the line.**

1. She hasn't eaten lunch ~~already~~.   _She hasn't eaten lunch yet._

2. All the students are yet here.   _____

3. Have you finished the book already?   _____

4. They haven't come home yet.   _____

5. A: Are you ready?

   B: No, not already.   _____

6. He has found already his wallet.   _____

7. The baby is already asleep.   _____

8. We yet haven't studied Chapter 8.   _____

4 Read the telephone bill and answer the questions.

Billing Date: Feb. 10
Account Number: 9555-6524-2221S
Account Name: Aslan, Ali

GENERAL TELEPHONE

BILLING SUMMARY	
Local Services	
Basic Local Service	$15.00
Total Local Usage	$5.75
Long Distance Services	
Long Distance Charges	$14.05
Federal Taxes	$1.65
Local Taxes	$0.75
Surcharges and Fees	$8.79
Current Charges	$45.99
Balance From Last Bill	$19.90
Total	**$65.89**

Previous Bill _____ $69.90
Payment _____ $50.00CR
Balance _____ $19.90

Current Charges _____ $45.99

Due in full by March 10.
Late payment penalty Begins March 15.

Payment to:
General Telephone, Inc.
P.O. Box 0853
Miami, FL 33126

1. Ali should pay this bill before _____ .
   a. February 10   b. March 10   c. March 15
2. The total bill is _____ .
   a. $45.99   b. $69.90   c. $65.89
3. Ali's last bill was _____ .
   a. $45.99   b. $69.90   c. $50.00
4. What is the total expense for local calls? _____
   a. $20.75   b. $15.00   c. $5.75
5. How much tax will Ali pay? _____
   a. $8.69   b. $1.65   c. $2.40

5 Fill in the blanks. Use the words from the box.

therm	billing period	~~meter number~~
emergency service number	account number	baseline

I just received my gas bill and I'm trying to understand all the numbers.

1. The ____meter number____ is the number on the outside of the machine that measures how much gas we use every month.
2. The _____ is the one I call if there is a serious problem in the middle of the night.
3. The _____ is the standard way of measuring heat energy.
4. The _____ is the exact dates that we used the gas.
5. The _____ is the number the gas company gave me. It's different from anyone else's number.
6. The _____ is an average amount of gas we use every month.

Erika's New Job

① Read each paragraph. Then choose the main idea.

1. Sometimes real estate agents make a lot of money. In some places they get 10%–15% of the first year's rental. That means up to $1,600 as a fee for renting a $900 apartment. If an agent rents one apartment a week, that's $83,200 a year! And the fee for selling a $100,000 condo can be as much as $6,000. On the other hand, when the market is slow, an agent might be able to rent only one or two apartments a month. And a condo might take eight or ten months to sell.

The main idea of this paragraph is:

   a. Apartment rental fees are high.

   b. Real estate agents can sell and rent apartments.

   c. A real estate agent's income can go up and down.

2. A real estate agent has just shown you the apartment of your dreams. It's old, but it has big windows looking out over a street with lots of interesting stores and restaurants. There is a fireplace in the living room and a nice, old-fashioned kitchen with tile walls and a very big stove. And best of all, it's not expensive. But you should take another look. Will that interesting street be noisy at night? Will those big windows let in cold air? Does the fireplace actually work, or is it just to look at? Do the old appliances in that old-fashioned kitchen work well? Maybe you should take a second look.

The main idea of this paragraph is:

   a. Apartments with fireplaces and big windows are not always expensive.

   b. It's important to inspect an apartment carefully before signing a lease.

   c. Sometimes older apartments are nicer than new ones.

② Rearrange the words to make correct questions and statements.

1. (paint / the walls/ you / allowed / are / to)
   <u>Are you allowed to paint the walls?</u>

2. (not / double parking / allowed / is)
   _____

3. (clothes / hanging / allowed / on the balcony / isn't)
   _____

4. (we / allowed / to have / in the apartment / are / a dog)
   _____

5. (fine / having / is / a / cat)
   _____

❸ Number the lines of each conversation in the correct order.

1.

____ You're welcome.

____ My garbage disposal doesn't work.

_1_ I'm sorry to bother you.

____ OK. I'll send over our maintenance man.

____ That's OK. What's the problem?

____ Thank you very much.

2.

____ I see. I'll send over the exterminator tomorrow.

____ I'm sorry to bother you.

____ Thanks.

____ That's OK. What's the problem?

____ You're welcome.

____ There are cockroaches in my kitchen.

3.

____ When will you be here?

____ I'm having a problem with my toilet.

____ What's the problem? Is it leaking?

____ This afternoon. I'll call first.

____ No, it's backed up.

____ OK. I'll come over and look at it.

4.

____ The apartment is cold. The heat isn't working.

____ When will he come?

____ I'm sorry to bother you but I need someone to come to my apartment.

____ What's the problem?

____ OK. I'll send the maintenance man over.

____ I'll send him right now.

❹ Answer the questions. Use a gerund as the subject in each of your sentences. Use the verb *allow.*

1. A: Can I swim here after 9:00 P.M.?

   B: *No. Swimming isn't allowed after 9:00 P.M.* _____

2. A: Can I eat in the pool area?

   B: *Yes.* _____

3. A: Can I bring guests to the pool?

   B: *No.* _____

4. A: Can I walk my dog near the pool?

   B: *No.* _____

5. A: Can we have parties at the pool?

   B: *Yes.* _____

Review

❶ Bubble the correct answers.

a   b   c

1. We have lived in this apartment _____ 2002.
   a) from   b) since   c) for   ○ ○ ○

2. I _____ lived in a townhouse.
   a) haven't never   b) have never   c) never have   ○ ○ ○

3. Chicago isn't _____ New York City.
   a) as big as   b) big as   c) as big than   ○ ○ ○

4. You will see the word "therms" on a _____.
   a) rent bill   b) telephone bill   c) utility bill   ○ ○ ○

5. _____ trash in the hall isn't allowed.
   a) Leave   b) Leaving   c) To leave   ○ ○ ○

6. You will see the abbreviation "sec. dep." _____.
   a) on an electricity bill b) on a credit card bill   c) in a rental ad   ○ ○ ○

❷ Fill in the blanks. Use the words from the box.

| leaks | qualify for | negotiable | down payment | ~~value~~ |
| equity | heating | roaches | $10,000 | |

    Dale and Helen are trying to decide whether to buy a house or rent one. They know that the (1) _____value_____ of any house they buy will go up. They like the idea of buying a home so that they can build some (2) _____. However, they are not sure if they will (3) _____ a mortgage or not. They know that they will have to make a 5 percent (4) _____. They have found a house that they like for $200,000. The price is (5) _____ so they may be able to pay less. Their down payment on this house would be (6) _____. That's a lot of money! Sometimes they think about renting a house. Then they wouldn't have to fix (7) _____, (8) control _____, or provide adequate (9) _____. They are going to have to think hard about this decision.

Vocabulary

Dentist	Pediatrics	Dermatology	Orthopedic Surgery
Obstetrics/Gynecology	Cardiology	Radiology	Internal Medicine

1 **Write the name of the medical office each person should go to.**

1. _Internal Medicine_   My grandmother has a fever.

2. _____ My wife is pregnant.

3. _____ My son hurt his arm. We don't know if it's broken or not.

4. _____ My son broke his arm in three places.

5. _____ I have high cholesterol.

6. _____ I need a skin cancer screening.

7. _____ My five-year-old daughter has an ear infection.

8. _____ I have a toothache.

9. _____ My wife has high blood pressure.

10. _____ I need a medical checkup.

2 **Which of these medical offices have you visited in the past year? Why did you visit them?**

_____

_____

_____

_____

_____

_____

_____

_____

_____

Staying Healthy

1 **Number the lines of each conversation in the correct order.**

1.

____ You ought to eat more vegetables.

_1_ I'm trying to lose weight. What should I do?

____ It would make your diet healthier.

____ First you should stop eating ice cream.

____ OK. That's one thing I can do. What else?

____ Why vegetables?

2.

____ Well, doctors recommend aerobic exercise five times a week.

____ That sounds very healthy. Did you exercise?

____ Lots of vegetables and very little meat.

____ I've tried a healthy diet but I didn't lose weight.

____ What did you eat?

____ No, I didn't.

3.

____ My doctor has office hours tomorrow.

____ Will that really help?

____ I can't fall asleep at night. What should I do?

____ Why don't you call her right now?

____ You ought to drink warm milk.

____ It should help, but maybe you should see a doctor.

4.

____ Well, I can do that.

____ Why don't you keep him in bed for a few days?

____ Should I take him to my doctor?

____ And maybe he ought to see a doctor.

____ My son has the flu. What should I do?

____ No, you should see a pediatrician.

5.

____ Then you ought to start.

____ Do you exercise?

____ No, I don't.

____ You should also try to get more sleep.

____ OK. That's one thing I can do.

____ I want to reduce my stress level.

6.

____ I have the hiccups.

____ Another idea is to breathe in and out slowly.

____ I tried that. It didn't work.

____ OK, I'll try that.

____ It usually works for me.

____ Why don't you drink a glass of water slowly?

❷ Circle the correct words in each question.

1. How much exercise (**have you done** / **did you do**) so far this week?

2. (**Have you taken** / **Did you take**) your vitamins yet today?

3. (**Have you eaten** / **Did you eat**) fast food yesterday?

4. How many hours (**have you slept** / **did you sleep**) last night?

5. (**Have you been** / **Were you**) sick so far this month?

6. How many times (**have you seen** / **did you see**) the dentist so far this year?

❸ Read the paragraph and complete Isabel's health survey.

Isabel hasn't been feeling well lately and she wants to have a healthier life. In the past month she has felt stressed every single day. She sleeps a lot because she thinks it will make her feel better. Every night she sleeps nine or ten hours. She has had four or five serious arguments with her husband and she's worried about that. She quit smoking two years ago, but she has started smoking every day again. She exercises two days a week, but maybe that isn't enough. She tried to meditate, but she couldn't do it. She knows that's not the way to solve her problems.

HealthNorth Medical Center

Health Survey

Name: _Isabel Nazario_   Doctor: _____

In the last 30 days, how many days have you . . .

1. smoked cigarettes?   _____

2. felt very stressed?   _____

3. meditated?   _____

4. slept less than five hours?   _____

5. slept more than nine hours?   _____

6. gone out with friends?   _____

7. done aerobic exercise?   _____

8. gotten very angry with someone?   _____

---

❹ What advice would you give Isabel?

_____

_____

_____

The Doctor's Office

❶ Match each symptom with a medical problem.

Symptoms

1. I have no energy and I can't sleep at night. __d__
2. My child has a rash all over her body. ____
3. Louis has a high fever and bad body aches. ____
4. Frank has a very bad stomachache and a fever. ____
5. Karen is dizzy and has chest pains. ____
6. Tim has a lot of pain in his wrist and can't move it. ____
7. My child has a fever and his ear hurts. ____
8. David has a BMI of 40. ____

Medical problems

a. a broken bone
b. the flu
c. appendicitis
d. ~~depression~~
e. a heart problem
f. measles
g. an ear infection
h. overweight

❷ Rewrite each conversation. Correct the underlined words. Use the words from the box.

~~cardiologist~~	heart	blood pressure	symptoms

1.

A: I'd like to see the <u>radiologist,</u> please.

B: What are your <u>infections</u>?

A: I get tired when I climb stairs. I can't breathe.

B: Have you had <u>ear</u> problems in the past?

A: No, but my <u>appendicitis</u> is very high.

B: Please have a seat. The doctor will see you soon.

A: _I'd like to see the cardiologist, please._

B: _____

A: I get tired when I climb stairs. I can't breathe.

B: _____

A: _____

B: Please have a seat. The doctor will see you soon.

a fever	rash	dermatologist	glands

2.

A: I think I have the measles.

B: Do you have swollen <u>hands</u>?

A: No, but I have a red <u>ache</u> on my chest.

B: Well, maybe it's not the measles.

A: Well, I don't have <u>an infection.</u> My temperature is 98.5°.

B: I think you should see a <u>dentist</u> about your skin.

A: I think I have the measles.

B: _____

A: _____

B: Well, maybe it's not the measles.

A: _____

My temperature is 98.5°.

B: _____

❸ Read the paragraph and complete the medical history form.

My name is Anton Damon, and Doctor Abrahams says I'm a healthy guy. I don't have asthma, cancer, or any cardiological problems. I have had an AIDS test and allergy tests, and there are no problems there. I never get headaches and I don't have diabetes. But my back has often been sore the past five years and the doctor says I have a little arthritis. I see a dermatologist every month for a rash around my eyes. I've never had surgery. I'm not allergic to any medications and I have never seen a doctor for mental problems. All in all, I'm in pretty good shape!

Medical History Form

NAME: _Anton Damon_____   DOCTOR: _____

INSURANCE: _SEGNA_____   DATE: _August 12, 2006_____

Have you ever had any of the following medical problems? (Answer Yes or No.)

high blood pressure ____	cancer ____	diabetes ____
heart disease ____	AIDS ____	arthritis ____
asthma ____	allergies ____	severe headaches ____

Are you currently under a doctor's care for any health problem? (If yes, what is the problem and how long have you had it?)

_____

Have you ever had a major operation? (If yes, explain.)

_____

Are you allergic to any medications? _____

If yes, which ones? _____

Have you ever been under the care of a mental health professional? (Explain.)

_____

---

❹ Check the childhood immunizations that children can receive.

____ polio   ____ AIDS

____ measles   ____ chickenpox

____ cancer   ____ hepatitis B

____ mumps   ____ appendicitis

⑤ Complete the lists with words from the box. Use each word once.

stomach	bones	~~heart~~	liver
muscles	arteries	eyes	intestines
ears	veins	blood	lungs

1. In the chest

heart _____

_____

2. Below the chest

_____

_____

_____

3. Everywhere

_____

_____

_____

_____

_____

4. Head

_____

_____

⑥ Read the paragraph and fill in the missing information on the form.

I have good insurance coverage. I even have my daughter, Anna, on the policy. Dr. Abrahams works with two other doctors. They call themselves ReadyDocs Inc. I have to pay the first $500 of medical expenses and then the policy pays the rest. If I need to go to the emergency room, I pay only $20 and drugs are $10 for brand name and $5 for generic. Each office visit I pay $5 with no deductible. I pay 20% of X-ray costs and 25% of hospital costs. If my wife has a baby, we only pay 10% of the cost. Cancer screenings are free. One thing worries me, though. We can't collect more than $2,000,000 in our lifetimes.

Medical Insurance, Inc.

Anton Damon   Member ID: 3990220393-01

Coverage includes _____ _____
                          (name)   (relationship)

Group: 4948-B

Medical Office: _____   Telephone: _(917) 555-6980_

Annual deductible: _____

Medical Plan Co-Pay: Office Visit: _____   (_____ deductible)
Covered Prescriptions: Generic $_____   Brand name $_____ (if generic available)
Emergency Room: _____
Professional Services: _____% (X-ray, blood tests, lab, etc.)
Hospital: _____% of total cost

Maternity: _____%
Preventive Care: $_____ for basic screenings (mammograms, cancer screenings, etc.)
Lifetime Maximum: _____

Safety

① Circle the correct word or words in each sentence.

1. Cleaning up trash helps prevent (**robberies / fires**).

2. If an accident happens, someone has to write a (**rule / report**).

3. A first aid kit is useful when someone is (**in danger / hurt**).

4. If there is a car accident, call (**a doctor / 911**).

5. If there is a fire, look for the nearest (**extinguisher / smoke alarm**).

6. A sign that says (**No smoking / No running**) helps prevent swimming pool injuries.

② Classify the underlined prepositions. Write *L* for prepositions of *location* and *M* for prepositions of *motion*.

1. __L__ The first aid kit is <u>above</u> the sink.

2. ____ The swimming pool is <u>between</u> the two buildings.

3. ____ The dog ran <u>around</u> the pool.

4. ____ The man fell <u>down</u> the stairs.

5. ____ There is a tall tree <u>next to</u> the apartment building.

6. ____ I drove <u>around</u> the block looking for a parking space.

7. ____ The boys jumped <u>into</u> the swimming pool.

8. ____ Please park your car <u>under</u> the building.

③ Describe an unsafe situation you have seen recently. Use prepositions of location and direction in your description.

_____

_____

_____

_____

_____

_____

4 **Respond to each statement with a second statement. Use** *should/shouldn't be + -ing* **verb or** *should/shouldn't +* **prepositional phrase.**

1. He is running in the hall.

   He shouldn't be running in the hall.

2. The child's parents are not at home at night.

   They should be home at night.

3. She is driving without a license.

   _____

4. They are smoking cigarettes at school.

   _____

5. It's cold and you're not wearing a coat.

   _____

6. It's midnight. The baby is in the living room.

   _____

7. It's 9:00 and the teacher isn't in the classroom yet.

   _____

8. They are running around the swimming pool.

   _____

9. She's pregnant and she's drinking alcohol.

   _____

10. The lifeguard isn't at the swimming pool.

   _____

5 **Think of a crime report you saw on television, heard on the radio, or read about in the newspaper. Write down as many of the details as you can remember by answering these questions.**

1. Where did it happen?   4. Who were the witnesses?

2. When did it happen?   5. What happened in the end?

3. Describe what happened.

_____

_____

_____

_____

_____

Review

① Bubble the correct answers.

	a	b	c

1. _____ quit smoking?
   a) You should   b) Why don't you   c) You ought to   ○ ○ ○

2. I _____ three fruits so far today.
   a) have eaten   b) should be eating   c) ate   ○ ○ ○

3. _____ is an example of a childhood disease.
   a) Pediatrics   b) Arthritis   c) Rubella   ○ ○ ○

4. Childhood immunizations should start at _____ of age.
   a) two years   b) two months   c) four years   ○ ○ ○

5. If you have the flu, you probably have _____.
   a) a bad earache   b) a sore arm   c) a high fever   ○ ○ ○

6. You body mass index shows if you _____.
   a) are overweight   b) have cancer   c) have appendicitis   ○ ○ ○

② Read each sentence. Choose the most likely inference.

1. __c__   Celia eats a lot of fruits and vegetables, exercises every day,
   and sees the doctor twice a year.

   a. She has food poisoning.
   b. She probably smokes.
   c. She is trying to live a healthy lifestyle.

2. ____   Barry never eats anything made with eggs.

   a. Eggs are too expensive.
   b. He is allergic to eggs.
   c. He is depressed.

3. ____   Norma never takes her child to the doctor when he is sick.

   a. Norma doesn't have health insurance.
   b. Norma has never had a major operation.
   c. The child has had all his immunizations.

4. ____   Robert's leg muscles hurt.

   a. He has asthma.
   b. He did too much exercise.
   c. He has heart disease.

Vocabulary

1 **Label the pictures. Use the words from the box.**

car	train	bicycle	motorcycle	plane	bus

_____ _____ _____ _____ _____ _____

_____ _____ _____ _____ _____ _____

2 **Under the name of each vehicle, write *Personal* if it is *personal transportation* and *Public* if it is *public transportation*.**

3 **Circle the correct word in each sentence.**

1. You can zip in and out of traffic on a (**train /** **bicycle**).

2. If you drive to and from work, you (**commute / fly**).

3. I don't want to walk to school so I (**drive / take**) a bus.

4. People drive very slowly when there is a lot of (**traffic / transportation**).

5. If you are flying, you are on a (**plane / motorcycle**).

6. When you travel a long distance, you take a (**travel / trip**).

7. If you zip in and out, you are moving (**slowly / quickly**).

8. A bus is usually faster than a (**plane / bicycle**).

4 **What is your favorite form of transportation? Why?**

_____

_____

_____

Travel Plans

1 Match the sentences that have the same meaning.

1. It's an economical car. _b_
2. It moves very quickly. ____
3. It's an exciting car. ____
4. It's a safe car. ____
5. It's a comfortable car. ____
6. It's a cheap car. ____
7. It's interesting. ____
8. It's public. ____
9. It's personal. ____
10. It's a good idea. ____

a. It isn't dangerous.
b. ~~It saves money.~~
c. It's not boring.
d. Only one person can use it.
e. It's fast.
f. I agree with you.
g. I can relax in it.
h. Everyone can use it.
i. It's a lot of fun.
j. It doesn't cost very much.

2 *Think* can be either an action verb or a nonaction verb. Label each sentence *A* if the underlined verb is an *action* verb, and *N* if it is a *nonaction* verb.

___N___ 1. Leon <u>thinks</u> that riding a bicycle is fun.

____ 2. We <u>think</u> that it might be a little dangerous.

____ 3. Leon <u>is thinking</u> about buying a bike.

____ 4. I <u>have been thinking</u> about selling him my old bike.

____ 5. What do you <u>think</u> of the idea?

____ 6. <u>Are you thinking</u> about buying a bike, too?

____ 7. Marta <u>thinks</u> that a motorcycle would be more fun.

____ 8. She <u>was thinking</u> about buying one last week.

____ 9. I <u>don't think</u> she should do that.

____ 10. I <u>am thinking</u> about how expensive it will be.

3 Rearrange the words to make correct statements and questions.

1. (California / thinking / they're / about / to / driving)

   They're thinking about driving to California.

2. (taken / you / have / ever / a bus)

   _____

3. (for / thinking / it / years/ been / about / we've)

   _____

4. (think / don't / I / good / it's / idea / a)

   _____

5. (thinking / doing / are / what / you / about / next summer)

   _____

6. (thinking / are / to Europe / of / you / going)

   _____

4 Circle the correct explanation for the underlined verb in each sentence.

1. I <u>have been waiting</u> for twenty minutes. Thank goodness you're finally here.

   a. The action is still going on.   (b.) The action has stopped.

2. I <u>have been studying</u> for two hours. I still have two more chapters to review.

   a. The action is still going on.   b. The action has stopped.

3. Ana <u>has been surfing the Internet</u> since 9:00 and still hasn't found the answer.

   a. The action is still going on.   b. The action has stopped.

4. I <u>have been trying</u> to find my wallet and here it is in my backpack!

   a. The action is still going on.   b. The action has stopped.

5. Linda <u>has been walking</u> for an hour and she still has two miles to go.

   a. The action is still going on.   b. The action has stopped.

5 Use the present perfect continuous to write about (1) a situation in your life that is still going on, and (2) a situation that has ended.

1. _____

   _____

2. _____

   _____

Getting There

❶ Complete each sentence.

1. A _f_ is coffee and a roll.
2. A ____ bed is bigger than a double bed.
3. A ____ includes eggs.
4. Do you have a room with a view ____ ?
5. A motel is the same as a ____.
6. I want to make a ____ at that new hotel.
7. Two hotel rooms together are called a ____.
8. A room for one person is called a ____.
9. I will need a credit card to ____ that room for you.
10. Let me ____. You want a single room on June 10th.

a. hold
b. single
c. reservation
d. available
e. king-size
f. ~~continental breakfast~~
g. confirm
h. full breakfast
i. suite
j. motor lodge

❷ Use *would rather* to write questions and answers.

1. A: _Would they rather have a single room or a double room?_____

   B: They'd prefer to have a single room.

2. A: _____

   B: I think I'd like a continental breakfast not a full breakfast.

3. A: Would you rather take a bus or a plane?

   B: _____

4. A: _Shall we visit New Orleans or San Francisco?_____

   B: _____

5. A: _____

   B: We would rather have a room with a view than a room in the back.

❸ Would you rather study a little every day or a lot the night before a big test? Which is smarter? Explain.

_____

_____

_____

4 Complete the driving directions.

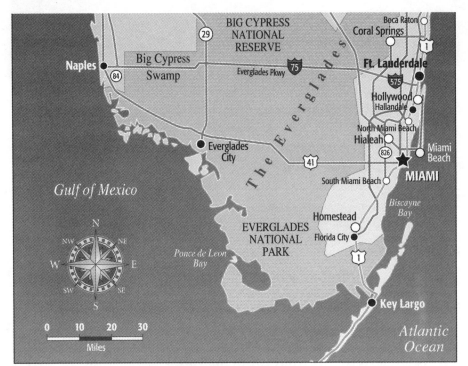

1. A: How can I get from Miami to Homestead?

   B: Take Highway 1 south to South Miami Beach. Then _____

   _____

2. A: How can I get from Miami to Everglades City?

   B: _____

   _____

3. A: How can I get from Miami to Naples?

   B: _____

   _____

5 Number the lines of the conversation in the correct order.

____ Do you have a double room available for April 11?

____ That's one room with a king-size bed for April 11. Would you like to hold that with a credit card?

_1_ Hello. May I speak to reservations, please?

____ This is reservations. How can I help you?

____ I'd rather have a king-size bed.

____ Sure.

____ Would you prefer double beds or a king-size bed?

Buying a Car

① Complete the lists with words from the box.

headlight	~~gas pedal~~	license plate	odometer	brake pedal	hubcap
side mirror	gas gauge	CD player	radio	hood	tire
clutch pedal	wheel	bumper	speedometer	glove compartment	

1. On the floor of a car

gas pedal _____

_____

_____

2. On the dashboard

_____

_____

_____

_____

_____

3. On the outside

_____

_____

_____

_____

_____

_____

② Circle the correct answer.

1. *Firm* means ____.

   (a.) not changing   b. very large

2. Most cars have ____ *cylinders*.

   a. 2 or 3   b. 4 or 6

3. *Mint* means ____.

   a. very new   b. very old

4. Most *transmissions* have ____ speeds.

   a. 3 or 4   b. 5 or 6

5. A word that describes a car's *condition* is ____.

   a. good   b. slow

6. The ____ connects to the *transmission*.

   a. odometer   b. gearshift

③ Complete each question or answer with one of the words in italics from Activity 2.

1. Q: That car looks really great!

   A: Yes, it's in ____*mint*____ condition.

2. Q: How many _____ does it have?

   A: Eight.

3. Q: I want $5,000 for the car.

   A: Is that a _____ price?

4. Q: Does it have an automatic _____?

   A: No, it doesn't.

4 **Complete the conversation. Describe your own car or a friend's car.**

A: I'd like to buy your _____. Is it still available?   (make of car)

B: Yes, it is.

A: Tell me a little about it.

B: It's a _____. It's got _____ and _____.   (year, cylinders, transmission)

A: How many miles does it have on it?

B: It has about _____.   (miles)

A: How many miles per gallon does it get?

B: It gets about _____.   (miles per gallon)

A: What else can you tell me about it?

B: _____ and _____.   (number of owners, condition)

A: And how much is the asking price?

B: It's _____.   (price)

A: Is that price flexible?

B: _____.   (yes or no)

5 **Answer the questions about the ads. Circle *True* or *False*.**

FOR SALE

2005 Wagon Master
Six cylinders. Manual transmission.
OK condition. Second owner.
23 mpg city. Seats 7 people.
$9,000 firm.

FOR SALE

2003 Tiger. Bright red sportscar.
Four cylinders. Automatic transmission.
Mint condition. 20 mpg city.
$10,000 or best offer.

1. You can offer $8000 for the Wagon Master.   True   (False)

2. The Wagon Master is bigger than the Tiger.   True   False

3. The Tiger is in better condition than the Wagon Master.   True   False

4. The Wagon Master is newer than the Tiger.   True   False

5. The Tiger gets better gas mileage than the Wagon Master.   True   False

6. You can offer $8000 for the Tiger.   True   False

6 Dale drove from New York City to Miami. Here is a record of his odometer readings and the amount of gasoline he used. Figure out how many miles per gallon he got during each part of his trip.

Location	Odometer reading	Miles traveled	Gallons of gas used	Miles per gallon
New York City	24,530			
(1) Washington, DC	24,770	240	8	30
(2) Columbia, SC	25,250	_____	18	_____
(3) Jacksonville, FL	25,550	_____	10	_____
(4) Miami, FL	25,900	_____	11	_____

7 Read the paragraph and fill in the missing information on the form.

My name is Susan Thomson and I am lucky to have very good insurance coverage on my car. I pay only $1,250 a year for my 2005 Tango LX. If the car is damaged in an accident, I only have to pay $250 for the repairs. If I should hurt people in another car, the insurance will pay each person up to $100,000. But they will only pay a total of $200,000 for any one accident. If I damage someone else's house or car, the company will pay $50,000 of the expenses. I think I have a pretty good deal!

Car World Insurance Company

Agent: Lee Gorman

Policy Number: D99-99-99hA

Policy Period: 3-31-05 to 3-31-06

Premium: $_____

Insured: Susan Thomson
333 Anderson Way
Cupertino, CA 90514

Covered Vehicle:

_____

VIN (Vehicle Identification Number): 7H327HG35487

Coverages: A - $750   B - $250   C - $250

A = Liability   **B= Collision**   **C= Comprehensive**

$_____ each person
$_____ each accident
$_____ property damage [each accident]

Review

1 **Bubble the correct answers.**

                                                                a   b   c

1. The odometer is usually near the _____.
   a) emergency brake   b) clutch   c) speedometer   ○ ○ ○

2. A person who is willing to change is _____.
   a) firm   b) flexible   c) economical   ○ ○ ○

3. I _____ fly than drive to Florida.
   a) rather would   b) rather   c) 'd rather   ○ ○ ○

4. I started studying at 10:00 this morning. I have been studying _____.
   a) for hours   b) since last week   c) yesterday   ○ ○ ○

5. The rearview mirror is at the _____ of the windshield.
   a) bottom   b) left   c) top   ○ ○ ○

6. When you call back to check on a hotel reservation, you are _____ the room.
   a) deducting   b) confirming   c) reserving   ○ ○ ○

2 **Read the story. Underline the most important parts. Then summarize the story in three sentences.**

> ### Biking Through Ireland
>
> Last summer I took a bicycle trip around Ireland. I had no idea what it was going to be like, but it was really great! I went with a group led by an Irish guide. Some of the hills were pretty steep, but the views at the top were worth it. The ocean is so blue and the sky so big and gray. There were also wonderful meals at local restaurants. I especially love the bread and cheeses—the best I've ever eaten! And I have one very special memory—a little boy about 5 years old stepped out into the road, put up his hand, and stopped all 12 of us in our tracks. We were so surprised. Then a minute later his mother came around the corner leading a flock of sheep. We all smiled at each other and I felt so happy. I'll remember that moment forever.
>
> —Michael Mancuso

1. _____

2. _____

3. _____

# Government and the Law

Chapter 9

Vocabulary

❶ Complete the sentences. Choose one word from each box.

traffic	~~speed~~	selective	tax	driver's	motor

license	service	~~limit~~	return	vehicle	regulations

1. You should never drive faster than the posted __speed__ __limit__.
2. You need a _____ _____ to drive a car.
3. If you want to be safe when you're driving, obey all the _____ _____.
4. A car is one type of _____ _____.
5. Every April a worker must complete a _____ _____.
6. Right now the _____ _____ only applies to men, not women.

❷ Circle the correct word or words in each sentence.

1. All men must (**apply to /** **register for**) the selective service.
2. They must do this when they (**get / reach**) age 18.
3. I hope I don't (**need / owe**) any taxes this year.
4. How old do you have to be to (**buy / reach**) cigarettes?
5. Did you ever (**register / fill out**) an income tax return?
6. How old do you have to be to (**get / apply to**) married?
7. Will you (**reach for / vote in**) the next election?
8. Do traffic laws (**apply to / owe**) everyone?

❸ Describe a law where you live now that is different in another state or country. Do you think the law here or in the other place is better? Explain.

_____

_____

_____

❶ Complete each sentence with the correct ending.

1. If you are in a car accident, you must call __e__ .
2. Your insurance company will ask you to fill out ____ .
3. You won't need an accident report if you don't have ____ .
4. If you do something very bad, you may receive ____ .
5. If you get a summons, you will have to go ____ .
6. If you go to court, you may want to bring ____ .
7. Each year a worker has to file ____ .
8. If you need help with a tax return, you can hire ____ .
9. At age 18, most students graduate from ____ .
10. The law requires young children to stay in ____ .

a. to court
b. a tax return
c. high school
d. school
e. ~~the police~~
f. a serious accident
g. an accident report
h. an accountant
i. a lawyer
j. a summons

❷ Write three sentences about each picture. Tell what the person *must do, must not do,* and *doesn't have to do.* Use your own ideas.

1.

2.

He must go to work today.

_____

_____

_____

_____

_____

❸ Complete the sentences. Choose one word or phrase from each box.

| go   pay   get | evicted   rent   a ticket   expelled   sued   to jail |

1. If you smoke in class, you can ___get___ ___expelled___ from school.
2. If you steal a lot of money, you can _____ _____ .
3. If you live in an apartment you have to _____ _____ .
4. If your dog bites someone, you can _____ _____ .
5. If you park on the sidewalk, you can _____ _____ .
6. If you don't pay your rent, you can _____ _____ .

4 Write the letter of the correct word or words in each blank.

1. You _a_ wear your heavy coat. It _c_ get a lot colder later on.

   a. had better   b. had better not   c. could

2. You ____ park there. You ____ get a ticket.

   a. had better   b. had better not   c. could

3. You ____ cross in the middle of the block, but you ____.

   a. had better   b. had better not   c. could

4. You ____ study a lot or you ____ fail the test.

   a. had better   b. had better not   c. could

5. You ____ drive 90 miles per hour, but you ____. You don't want to get arrested.

   a. had better   b. had better not   c. could

5 Rearrange the words to make correct warnings.

1. (leave / in the car/ don't / your / keys)   _Don't leave your keys in the car._

2. (argue / classmates / don't / your / with)   _____

3. (bring / to school / don't / drugs)   _____

4. (cheat / don't / your / on / taxes)   _____

5. (don't / without / drive / license / a)   _____

6. (job / your / steal / don't / on)   _____

7. (drive / car / without / insurance / don't / a)   _____

8. (cross / in the / block / don't / of the / middle)   _____

6 Match each warning in Activity 5 with a consequence below.

1. _4_ You could pay interest and penalties.

2. ____ You could get fired.

3. ____ You could lose your driver's license.

4. ____ You could have it stolen.

5. ____ You could get kicked out of class.

6. ____ You could get a jaywalking ticket.

7. ____ You could get expelled from school.

8. ____ You could get arrested for not having one.

❼ Write the approximate age of students at each level of education.

1. Pre-K   _3 to 4 years_

2. Kindergarten   _____

3. Elementary School   _____

4. Middle School (Junior High School)   _____

5. High School (Secondary School)   _____

6. College or University   _____

7. Graduate School (Professional School)   _____

❽ Complete each sentence with the correct ending.

1. A teacher isn't allowed to __d__ .

2. If parents don't like the local public school, they can ____.

3. At some schools students look the same because they ____.

4. Twice a year most students ____.

5. Children can't start kindergarten unless they ____.

6. All children less than 16 years old must ____.

7. A school system isn't allowed to ____.

8. It is dangerous for children to ____.

9. If you finish college, you usually ____.

10. After a child is 16 years old, he or she can ____.

a. quit school

b. get a bachelors degree

c. discriminate against children because of race

d. ~~hit a child~~

e. take standardized tests

f. wear uniforms every day

g. bring weapons to school

h. attend school

i. receive immunizations

j. choose a private school

❾ Write several sentences comparing traffic laws in the U.S. to the traffic laws in your country. Tell how they are the same and how they are different.

_____

_____

_____

_____

_____

Citizenship

Lesson 2

1 Read the statements about the U.S. flag. Circle *True* or *False*.

1. The stripes represent the number of original states. (True) False
2. There is sometimes an eagle on a U.S. flagpole. True False
3. There are 13 red stripes on the U.S. flag. True False
4. The U.S. flag has four colors. True False
5. There are 48 stars on the U.S. flag. True False
6. The U.S. flag is called the Star Spangled Banner. True False

2 Circle the names of the United States presidents.

Denzel Washington	Thomas Jefferson	Michael Jackson	Franklin D. Roosevelt
Ulysses S. Grant	Alexander Hamilton	(Abraham Lincoln)	George Washington
John F. Kennedy	Andrew Jackson	Robert F. Kennedy	George Jefferson

3 Number the steps to apply for citizenship in the correct order.

____ Fill out the application.

_1_ Pick up an application from a counselor.

____ Look up any information you don't remember.

____ Bring the application back to your counselor.

____ Call your counselor to see if the application is complete.

____ Make sure you understand everything on the application.

____ Get the completed application from your counselor.

____ Mail the application to the INS.

____ The counselor will check over your application.

4 Rewrite each sentence. Use one of the phrasal verbs in the box.

| wait for | ~~bring back~~ | go over | pick up | read through | find out | call up | look up |

1. Please return my dictionary tomorrow.   _Please bring back my dictionary tomorrow._
2. Please stay until Shelia arrives.   _____
3. I need to learn more about the problem.   _____
4. I'll find the number in the phone book.   _____
5. We'll review the correct answers.   _____
6. Please get some milk at the supermarket.   _____
7. Where can I get the answer?   _____
8. I will read the story quickly.   _____

5 Cross out the incorrect part of the sentence. Then rewrite the sentence correctly. If the sentence does not have any mistakes, write *correct* on the line.

1. I will ~~look it into~~.   _I will look into it._
2. I will look up it in the dictionary.   _____
3. Please bring it back tomorrow.   _____
4. Please wait me for at the corner.   _____
5. I sent back it to the bank.   _____
6. You can pick up it on Friday.   _____
7. Please read it through before class.   _____
8. We will go it over in class later.   _____

History and Government

Lesson 3

1 **Label each branch of the government under the picture. Then complete the lists with words from the box. Use each word once.**

members appointed by the president   two houses   ~~president~~   cabinet
Supreme Court   vice president   Congress   commander-in-chief   judges
Senate   over 400 members   interpret the Constitution

1. *Executive branch*

president

_____

_____

_____

_____

2. _____

_____

_____

_____

_____

_____

3. _____

_____

_____

_____

_____

_____

2 **Use the numbers in the box to answer the questions. You will use the number 2 three times and the number 4 two times.**

| 2 | 3 | 4 | 9 | 435 |

1. There are __2__ major political parties in the U.S.

2. There are ____ members of Congress.

3. Independence Day is July ____.

4. There are ____ houses of Congress.

5. Each state has ____ Senators.

6. There are ____ Supreme Court Justices.

7. The president is elected for ____ years.

8. There are ____ branches of the U.S. federal government.

3 **Rearrange the words to express agreement or disagreement. Then label each sentence A for *agreement* or D for *disagreement*.**

1. (so / think / I / don't)   *I don't think so.*   __D__

2. (too / thinks/ she / so)   _____   ____

3. (doesn't / so / think / he)   _____   ____

4. (they / so / think / too)   _____   ____

4 Number the lines of the conversation in the correct order.

____ I think he was a Democrat.

____ Maybe you're right. Was Kennedy a Democrat or a Republican?

_1_ Who was the president in 1962?

____ No, I don't think so. I think John Kennedy was president in 1962.

____ I think so too.

____ I think Lyndon Johnson was.

5 Circle the correct answers.

1. Election day is in ____.

   (a.) November   b. December   c. January

2. A president can be elected for ____ terms.

   a. 2   b. 3   c. 4

3. The author of the Declaration of Independence was ____.

   a. George Washington   b. Abraham Lincoln   c. Thomas Jefferson

4. Each state has ____ Senators in Congress.

   a. six   b. three   c. two

5. The Declaration of Independence was written in ____.

   a. 1620   b. 1776   c. 1802

6. The first president of the United States was ____.

   a. George Washington   b. Abraham Lincoln   c. Thomas Jefferson

6 Answer as many of the following questions as you can.

1. Who was president of the U.S. the year you were born? _____

2. Who is the current president?   _____

3. What state is the president from?   _____

4. Who is your state's governor?   _____

5. Who is your Congressperson?   _____

Review

❶ Bubble the correct answers.

	a	b	c

1. The House of Representatives has _____ than the Senate.
   a) fewer members than   b) more members than   c) the same number of members as   ○ ○ ○

2. Religious schools are one type of _____ school.
   a) private   b) public   c) government   ○ ○ ○

3. All males must _____ when they reach 18.
   a) file an income tax return   b) vote in an election   c) register for the selective service   ○ ○ ○

4. You received a summons. You _____ go to court.
   a) could   b) don't have to   c) have to   ○ ○ ○

5. If you are under 18 years old, you are _____.
   a) a bachelor   b) a minor   c) self-employed   ○ ○ ○

6. The federal government gets money through _____.
   a) tax returns   b) the selective service   c) driver's licenses   ○ ○ ○

Critical Thinking:

Some students cheat on tests, argue with other students, or bring drugs to school. Write a short paragraph telling what you think schools should do with students like these. Should they be kicked out of class? Should the school expel them? Why or why not? What do you think schools can do to help these students become better people?

_____

_____

_____

_____

_____

_____

_____

_____

_____

Vocabulary

1 Rewrite the underlined part of each sentence. Use the expressions from the box. Use capital letters as needed.

would you mind   of course   I don't mind   would you get that   ~~if you don't mind~~

1. Would you mail this letter on your way to work <u>if it isn't too much trouble?</u>

   Would you mail this letter on your way to work *if you don't mind?* _____

2. It's no problem. <u>I'm happy to do it</u>.

   It's no problem. _____ at all.

3. <u>Would it be a problem for you to</u> pick up the children after school for me?

   _____ picking up the children after school for me?

4. <u>Would you answer that phone</u>, please?

   _____, please?

5. <u>Certainly</u>. I'd be glad to.

   _____ I'd be glad to.

2 Complete each question with the correct ending.

1. Could you please take __f__?
2. Would you please clean up that ____?
3. Should I mop the ____?
4. When will they deliver the ____?
5. Do you like to get ____?
6. Is that part of your ____?
7. Does she always stay ____?
8. Are you an apprentice ____?
9. What was that polite ____?
10. Would you mind answering the ____?

a. phone
b. mechanic
c. busy
d. package
e. expression he used
f. ~~a message~~
g. mess
h. floor
i. outside at lunchtime
j. job

Working Together

❶ Number the lines of each conversation in the correct order.

1.

____ OK. I'll get it.

_1_ Can I help you with anything?

____ Yes, the one with the black handle.

____ Thank you.

____ No problem.

____ Knife?

____ Yes, please. Could you get me that knife over there?

2.

____ OK. Do you need anything else from there?

____ Could you take this package to the post office for me?

____ OK. I'll drop off the package and get stamps.

____ You're welcome.

____ Could you do me a favor?

____ Sure. What is it?

____ Yes. Please get some stamps at the same time.

____ Thanks.

❷ Copy sentences from the conversations in Activity 1 in the correct column below.

Requests for help

Could you get me that knife over there?

_____

_____

Offers of help

_____

_____

❸ Complete each sentence with the correct word or phrase from the box.

| rental | ~~yellow~~ | rules | fine point | manila | return | listings |

1. You can find the phone number in the _____yellow_____ pages.

2. It's in the business _____.

3. We had to sign a _____ agreement for our apartment.

4. There were lots of _____ in the agreement.

5. We signed the agreement with a _____ pen.

6. We put the agreement in a _____ envelope.

7. We remembered to put the _____ address on the envelope.

4 Circle the correct answers.

1. There is ____ book on the table. Is it yours?

   a. a   b. an   c. the

2. How difficult was ____ test yesterday?

   a. a   b. an   c. the

3. California is ____ state.

   a. a   b. an   c. the

4. It is ____ hour until class begins.

   a. a   b. an   c. the

5. Lisa is ____ student.

   a. a   b. an   c. the

6. My aunt is ____ actress.

   a. a   b. an   c. the

7. ____ food at Frank's Pizzeria is great!

   a. A   b. An   c. The

8. Where does ____ president of the college live?

   a. a   b. an   c. the

5 Circle the correct pronoun in each sentence.

1. A: Could you do (**me** / **myself**) a favor?

2. B: Sure. What do (**yours** / **you**) need?

3. A: Could you ask Karen to call me if you see (**her** / **hers**)?

4. B: OK. I'll tell (**herself** / **her**).

   A: Anything else?

5. B: Could you give Jack this book? It's (**him** / **his**).

6. A: Sure. I'll give it to (**he** / **him**).

7. B: I would do it (**mine** / **myself**), but I'm really busy.

   A: No problem.

8. B: Tell (**he** / **him**) I'll talk to him tomorrow.

6 **Rewrite each sentence. Replace the underlined words with the correct pronoun.**

1. The book with the blue cover is <u>your book</u>.

   The book with the blue cover is yours.

2. They will do the job <u>without any help</u>.

   _____

3. Please give this envelope to <u>your sister</u>.

   _____

4. The supervisor said I should give it to <u>Bob and Ellen</u>.

   _____

5. That red pen is <u>my pen</u>.

   _____

6. Roberto carried the heavy box <u>all alone</u>.

   _____

7. This is <u>your coat</u>, isn't it?

   _____

8. I hope <u>you and I</u> aren't late to work.

   _____

7 **What home or office jobs such as using a dishwasher or sending a fax do you know how to do? Write a set of instructions for a task like these.**

_____

_____

_____

_____

_____

_____

Rules at Work

1 **Read the memo. Then write sentences about how the employees should behave at work.**

Dress For Less, Inc.

TO: All employees
FROM: Frank Costa
RE: Work habits that need improvement

Most of you have been doing a great job and our sales figures prove it! However, I have noticed that some people could do more to make *Dress For Less* an even more successful company. Please read the following list. If any of the comments applies to you, please see what you can do to improve your behavior.

1. Some people speak Spanish on the job all the time.
2. Several employees are late to work more than once a week.
3. Several clerks have been making personal calls at work.
4. Some employees have been taking 45-minute breaks.
5. Some workers have been arguing with coworkers.
6. Several clerks have been rude to customers.
7. Some employees have been wearing jeans and T-shirts to work.

---

1. _They should speak English on the job._ _____
2. _____
3. _____
4. _____
5. _____
6. _____
7. _____

2 **Complete each sentence with *have got, have got to, has got,* or *has got to.***

1. We __have got__ three televisions at home.

2. She _____ go home now. It's late.

3. They _____ dress more professionally.

4. He _____ six brothers.

5. I _____ a bad headache.

6. You _____ study more.

3 Rearrange the words. Write the correct sentences below.

A: Ms. Slater, (speak / you / to / I / could / minute / a / for / ?)

Could I speak to you for a minute?

B: Sure. (do / can / you / for / what / I / ?)

_____

A: (apologize / to / like / I'd / for / old jeans / to work / wearing / .)

_____

(forgot / I / do / to / the laundry / .)

_____

B: (you / thank / apologizing / for / .)

_____

(important / is / professionally / dressing / here / .)

_____

A: (won't / it / again / happen / .)

_____

B: Good. (that / hear / glad / to / I'm / .)

_____

(you / for / thank / in / coming / .)

_____

4 Write two personal apologies. Follow each with an explanation.

Example: *I'd like to apologize for not calling you last night. I got very busy with the children*
and forgot.

_____

_____

_____

_____

5 Rewrite the sentences correctly.

1. I am looking forward going home soon.   *I am looking forward to going home soon.*

2. They are thinking about go to the movies. _____

3. Are you interested learning French?   _____

4. I want to thank you for let me use your calculator. _____

5. I am tired to walking to work every day. _____

6. I want to apologize for be late yesterday. _____

Job Performance

1 Study the performance evaluations. Then answer the questions.

Performance Evaluation Form

NAME: _Simon Davidson_

SUBJECT	RATING	NOTES
Attendance:	_F_	_2 sick days, 6 personal days_
Punctuality:	_F_	_late 10 times_
Skills:	_O_	_excellent job skills_
Work Habits:	_E_	
Sociability:	_O_	
Appearance:	_P_	_does not dress professionally_
Overall Rating:	_F_	

Recommended for promotion? ___ YES   _✓_ NO

Rating Scale: Outstanding, Excellent, Good, Fair, Poor
A "Fair" or "Poor" rating indicates a problem that must be corrected within a six-month period.

Performance Evaluation Form

NAME: _Wanda Wolfley_

SUBJECT	RATING	NOTES
Attendance:	_E_	_0 sick days, 1 personal day_
Punctuality:	_G_	_late 2 times_
Skills:	_O_	_great computer skills_
Work Habits:	_G_	
Sociability:	_F_	
Appearance:	_E_	_very professional_
Overall Rating:	_G_	

Recommended for promotion? _✓_ YES   ___ NO

Rating Scale: Outstanding, Excellent, Good, Fair, Poor
A "Fair" or "Poor" rating indicates a problem that must be corrected within a six-month period.

---

1. Simon's employer is happy with his job performance.   True   (False)

2. Simon works hard on the job.   True   False

3. Simon's overall rating is good.   True   False

4. Simon will probably get a raise.   True   False

5. Wanda is usually punctual.   True   False

6. Wanda wears inappropriate clothes to work.   True   False

7. Wanda's work skills are outstanding.   True   False

8. Wanda is friendly with her coworkers.   True   False

2 **Should Simon try to keep his job or should he look for another one? Why? What should he do if he decides to stay at this job?**

_____

_____

_____

_____

3 **Summarize Wanda's job performance evaluation. Use three or four sentences.**

_____

_____

_____

_____

4 **Read the paragraph and complete the evaluation form. Use the ratings _O, E, G, F,_ and _P._ Add notes whenever possible.**

Overall, I'd have to say that Maryanne is a good worker. She wasn't late once this year and she only took two personal days. That's an outstanding record! However, her appearance needs work. She occasionally wears old clothes or things that aren't really professional. I'd say her appearance is only fair. Maryanne's work habits and skills are excellent. She is a fine computer programmer. And she's really friendly with her coworkers. She remembers everyone's birthday and often organizes parties.

SUBJECT	RATING	NOTES
Attendance:	_____	_____
Punctuality:	_____	_____
Skills:	_____	_____
Work Habits:	_____	_____
Sociability:	_____	_____
Appearance:	_____	_____
Overall Rating:	_____	_____

1 Bubble the correct answers.

a   b   c

1. He was late to work so he _____ the supervisor.
   a) thanked   b) apologized to   c) talked about   ○ ○ ○

2. I am thinking about _____ the day off.
   a) taking   b) to take   c) take   ○ ○ ○

3. It's cold. You _____ put on a coat.
   a) got to   b) have got   c) have got to   ○ ○ ○

4. I gave it to you. It's _____.
   a) your   b) yours   c) yourself   ○ ○ ○

5. Call Rita and tell _____ to bring her dictionary.
   a) she   b) her   c) herself   ○ ○ ○

6. I want to visit _____ Empire State Building.
   a) a   b) an   c) the   ○ ○ ○

2 Read the advice column. Then answer the questions.

Dear Ms. Know It All,

Well, New Years is almost here and everybody's talking about making resolutions. I think it's a terrible idea. The things they want to change probably should be changed, but that's not the way to do it. Most people fail to follow through, usually within two or three days! And then they feel worse about their bad habits than they did before. That makes it even harder for them to change. I'm against New Year's Resolutions!

—Unhappy Every New Year

Dear Unhappy Every New Year

Well, I think resolutions are a great idea. If it weren't for this one time of year, some people would never try to lose weight or quit smoking or start exercising. So maybe it doesn't work for some people some of the time, but at least it gets them thinking about making changes in their lives. And then maybe they'll try again later on. I say, "Go for it!"

—Ms. Know It All

Critical Thinking:

Do you usually make New Year's resolutions? How well do you follow through on them? What do you think of Ms. Know It All's advice? Do you agree or disagree? On a piece of paper, write your own letter of advice to *Unhappy Every New Year.*